"As a member of a leadership team going through a hundred-day transformation, I was indeed fortunate to learn the Canady approach, process, and tools firsthand, and to see how the interconnected parts of the methodology fueled alignment, urgency, and clarity as we moved rapidly toward profitable growth. We're now in our third year of deployment, and the strategy continues to build. Bill's book succinctly outlines the transformation journey with insight and humor. I recommend reading *The 80/20 CEO* as you start your own hundred days and then continue to use it as a reference all along the way. As the author often tells us, it's about progress, not perfection. Get 1 percent better each day."

> —Robert Wilson, President, Industrial Automation and Finishing at Ohio Transmission Corporation

"I am very impressed by just how much is packed into *The 80/20 CEO*. Anyone running a business—even more than one business—will be thrilled to have finally found an author who really gets it! As aspiring businesspeople trying to make their way in the world, we all encounter gurus who do little more than research and repeat. Bill Canady is a high cut above these because he has personally and successfully put 80/20 into real-world practice many times over. The writing here is pragmatic, disarmingly honest, and highly effective."

> —Ray Hoglund, Member, Board of Directors, Marcone Supply

"Seasoned CEO Bill Canady lays out a direct, systematic approach to creating profitable growth using data-driven analysis to identify what actions best drive an organization's growth. Especially valuable for PE-sponsored CEOs and their leadership teams, *The 80/20 CEO* will guide the leader of any enterprise in adopting an 'eyes wide open' approach to managing all the value streams of the organization. Canady's innovative 80/20 Profitable Growth Operating System (PGOS) clarifies and simplifies leadership action for profitable growth. A great, fast-paced, no-nonsense read."

—Jim Wisnoski, Retired CEO, Private Equity Advisor

"In *The 80/20 CEO*, Bill Canady shares his extensive experience to provide executives a comprehensive road map for profitable growth and improved strategic positioning. Blending pragmatism, stories, insights, and tips in a highly entertaining and refreshing style, Canady makes critical processes crystal clear and provides loads of practical, hands-on advice. Any executive or manager will benefit by adding this book's principles and guidance to their toolkit."

—Alan Fortier, President, Fortier & Associates Inc., and Director, Graham Corporation (GHM)

"Bill Canady's *The 80/20 CEO: Take Command of Your Business in 100 Days* is a playbook that can transform just about any business. Based on my own firsthand experience, I can attest that Canady's four-step PGOS process provides the best application of the Pareto Principle for improving profitability. His trade secrets for turning a business around are an invaluable bonus!"

—Monique Verduzco, SVP Strategy, Arrowhead Engineered Products

"I'm deeply impressed by *The 80/20 CEO: Take Command of Your Business in 100 Days*.

Canady shows how to apply the 80/20 process to lift your business to greater success in existing operations as well as in M&A. This is an invaluable guide to building strong management of personnel and operations. It will help you to improve the performance of managers and elevate product quality as well as profitability."

—Michael L. Hurt, Strategic Advisory Board, Genstar

"*80/20 CEO* is a game-changer, providing businesses with the fastest and most accurate methodology for transformation. Drawing on his wealth of experience, Bill Canady introduces a system that zeros in on the core elements crucial for success. The emphasis on the 80/20 principle ensures that efforts yield maximum impact, making it a powerful tool for any organization seeking growth. I've applied this system and have personally witnessed its transformative effects. It drives results. Canady's expertise shines through, making this book an indispensable guide for businesses aiming not just for change but for profitable and sustainable growth."

—Matt Marthinson, COO, OTC Industrial Technologies

"With sharp insights drawn from rich experience and a range of leadership roles, Bill Canady has written a detailed playbook for aspiring as well as accomplished senior-level executives seeking to lead their organizations to profitable strategic growth, and to do so on demand, on pace, and without surprises. Like its author, *The 80/20 CEO* is focused, observant, relatable, yet inspirational. As president of Elmhurst University—Bill's alma mater—I can attest to how much our institution has benefited from the knowledge and expertise he has shared as a member of our Board of Trustees and chair of the Investment Committee. I couldn't be more pleased that he is sharing that knowledge with new audiences through this timely book."

—Troy D. VanAken, PhD, President, Elmhurst University

"I have seen tremendous results at our portfolio companies under Bill Canady's leadership, most recently growing EBITDA by 150 percent in less than two and a half years. Not only is the PGOS system presented in *The 80/20 CEO* effective, it provides clarity, transparency, and alignment among operators, investors, and financing partners. What Bill's application of the 80/20 method brings to a company's strategic plan is extremely motivating. People are reinvigorated when they have a clear, logical plan producing measurable results."

—Deryn Jakolev, Principal at Genstar Capital

"The *80/20 CEO* is a holistic step-by-step approach to transforming an organization into a high-performing, highly profitable business. I've use Canady's Profitable Growth System, and it works!"

—Brett Stanton, President, Pump Motor Technology, OTC Industrial Products

The 80/20 CEO:
Take Command of Your Business in 100 Days

by Bill Canady

© Copyright 2024 Bill Canady

ISBN 979-8-88824-248-3

Published by

köehlerbooks™

3705 Shore Drive
Virginia Beach, VA 23455
800-435-4811
www.koehlerbooks.com

The
80/20
CEO

Take Command of Your Business
in 100 Days

BILL CANADY

VIRGINIA BEACH
CAPE CHARLES

To my wife Debbie,
your love and support has made it all possible.

CONTENTS

Author's Disclaimer

MUCH THAT I have written here is based on my executive and leadership experience working with various companies and individuals. In the interest of privacy and, even more, the protection of proprietary information, I have either avoided naming those companies by simply referring to them generically or, for convenience, supplied fictitious names.

—*Bill Canady*

PART I

What to Do First and What to Do Next

CHAPTER 1

Who Yuh Gonna Call?

"Depend upon it, sir, when a man knows he is to be hanged in a fortnight, it concentrates his mind wonderfully."

—SAMUEL JOHNSON

EVEN GOOD COMPANIES lose their way. When that happens, what do you need?

Profitable growth on demand. *Now*, in fact.

And who yuh gonna call?

The guy who's got the operating system. And since I'm that guy—*me*—you now have access to the profitable growth operating system (PGOS) playbook that will show you how to turn your business around in 100 days, use the 80/20 principle to earn the right to grow, and position it for long-term profitable growth. This book will walk you through all the strategic actions needed to prioritize everything possible on the 20 percent of investments, processes, products, and customers that generate 80 percent of your revenue. (80/20—that's a thing. And not just a thing; it's a natural law. Just 20 percent of what you do or spend generates 80 percent of your revenue. Don't get too happy, though, because the other 80 percent of what you spend generates just 20 percent of your revenue.)

Who Am I?

I grew up in southeastern North Carolina on a small farm in a double-wide trailer at the end of a dirt road. The nearest town, Richlands, had maybe a thousand residents, a couple or three traffic lights, two churches, and three saloons. My father created something resembling a living, working as a handyman, truck driver, and farm laborer. But feel free to assume that we were dirt poor—because we were.

There was an elementary school and a high school, thank goodness. I was aware of the existence of something called college, but when I graduated from high school, I had no idea how to get into such a place. My high school didn't have a college adviser. Well, that's not quite true. Set into a recess in the wall outside the office was a rack that held pamphlets on everything from vocational opportunities (big emphasis on "welders") to colleges (mostly local). That rack was our college adviser.

As I saw it, I had four choices after high school—and none of them were college.

1. I had a big mouth, so I could be a salesman.
2. I could learn some trade (hey, how about welding?).
3. I could be a farm laborer.
4. I could join the military.

This last one looked like the surest thing, so I enlisted in the US Navy for a three-year hitch. If modern fighting aircraft are computers that fly, modern fighting ships are computers that float, so I chose to do something with electronics in the Navy. Boot camp was at Great Lakes Naval Training Center a few miles north of Chicago, and after my specialty training, I served on the USS *Fort Fisher* (LSD-40), an *Anchorage*-class dock landing ship designed to support amphibious operations of all kinds. I chose wisely. Like every other sailor, I grumbled a lot, but the Navy was a great experience. It taught me much about basic leadership, introduced me to technology, and inculcated a respect for the power of process, procedure, and checklists. These were tools I never forgot. By way of a bonus, my three-year hitch showed me a slice of the wide world beyond Richlands.

When I got out of the Navy, I scored some low-level salesman jobs and then, one day, ran across a magazine dedicated to the HVAC (heating, ventilation, air-conditioning) industry. The back of the magazine was full of want ads, so, armed with my USN-trained background in hands-on technology maintenance, I applied to several companies and was called back by a filtration company that wanted a sales guy in the Midwest. I jumped at it, took the job, and moved to Naperville, a suburb just west of Chicago. I became a sales rep there, met my wife, and started a family.

My bride was a schoolteacher, which triggered my ambition to become something more than a salesman and a high school graduate. In hindsight, I took a very intentional, even strategic approach to growing and realizing my ambition. Having gotten a taste of business, I now wanted a leadership position in business. I figured that getting one of these required an MBA. Now, because I had a job and a family, I needed to earn that MBA locally while working full time. The best place to go—really, the only place I wanted to go—was the University of Chicago.

It was an objective easier declared than attained. Chicago was not and is not a pushover school, and its prestigious MBA program was and remains highly selective. For one thing, I needed to earn an undergraduate degree before even applying. (*Yuh think?*) For another, even if an applicant was amply qualified, the Chicago MBA program took only 5 percent of those who knocked at the gate.

Crash and Burn

The risk faced by everyone who tries to do something hard—from getting into an elite school to leading a business—is surprisingly similar to the risk of piloting an airplane. You could crash and burn. Ever wonder why most novice private pilots don't crash and burn the first time they solo?

Years ago, I made my first solo flight—from Waterloo, Iowa, bound for Dodge City, Kansas. All went well until I approached the airport, down around 1,200 feet on a hot summer afternoon. When I came in low over a pond adjacent to the field, the thermal reflecting off it shot me up maybe 200 feet.

"Holy shit," I said out loud to no one because I was the only one there. "I *am* going to die."

But then the steps of the final approach and landing process I had been taught, taught again, and taught some more unrolled in my mind, step by step, like the screen credits in a movie. My heart was racing. I was in a cold sweat in a very warm cockpit. But I went through all the motions, and the next thing I knew, I was bouncing on the welcoming tarmac as only a Cessna 150 in the hands of a rank rookie can bounce.

I landed. I stopped. I taxied.

No fiery death for me. Not this time.

Now, it's not that I had been taught to land. It's that I had been taught a *process for landing*. A "process" is to flying a plane what an OS is to working a computer. It gets between you and the machine so that you can make that digital hardware do exactly what you need it to do.

On the face of it, the odds were daunting, but I had a plan, procedure, and process. Possessing a plan, procedure, and process—an operating system—always helps to even the odds. You may already know that before Facebook became Facebook, it was The Facebook, which was started by Mark Zuckerberg when he was a Harvard undergrad (and future Harvard dropout). The Facebook was initially confined to Harvard students and alumni. Soon, other colleges and universities started their own Facebook branches, including Chicago. A buddy of mine, who was going to the University of Chicago, gave me his login credentials to log onto the university's Facebook. I searched it to identify where the current crop of MBA candidates had gone to undergraduate school. The highest number who had attended a school in the Chicago area—five individuals—came from Elmhurst College (today University). It turned out to be a good, serious school. A recent *U.S. News & World Reports Best Colleges Ranking* put it at number four in its "Best Value Schools in the Midwest." Anyway, it suited my three very particular needs to a tee:

1. It was local.
2. It was "value" priced.
3. By the numbers, it gave me a decent shot at getting into the MBA program at Chicago.
4. There were also a third and fourth dimension to my strategy: Selective as Chicago was, it was also extremely flexible. Entry into the graduate school would gain me admission into any course of study. So, there was more than one way to get onto the MBA track.
5. Chicago admissions placed great emphasis—more than most schools—on a personal interview. I was a very good salesman—confident, personable, and sincere. I was also precise and able to articulate what I intended to do with my MBA.

I graduated summa cum laude from Elmhurst in three years, and I aced the interview at Chicago. It was clear to the admissions committee that I was intensely focused. I was also older than the average applicant and had been in the working end of the business world. I was thrilled when Chicago said yes. (Incidentally, I was and remain very grateful to Elmhurst and today serve on its board as chairman of the Investment Committee. *Pay it forward!*)

The Chicago MBA proved to be a powerful credential. The university and its MBA program had a reputation for rigor, accountability, and a pragmatic, real-world focus. The unofficial motto of the institution is "University of Chicago: Where Fun Goes to Die." (In my day, many students wore sweatshirts or hoodies emblazoned with that creed.) There is truth and value to this sentiment, and straight out of grad school, I was hired as a product manager by a global tech company focusing on industrial automation and energy controls. This was a step down in salary from my sales job with the filtration company, but you cannot measure your journey toward a strategic goal strictly by the money you pull down at any step along the way. Sometimes, you need to take a step back to advance. In sales, I knew I could get only so far in the business universe. I also knew that sales is rarely the road to becoming a CEO. As a product manager, I was able to work my way up rapidly.

But in what kind of company was I making my climb?

At the time, the firm I worked for was a $26 billion company, but it was in deep trouble. Too many acquisitions too quickly were squeezing its margins. To make matters worse, it was embroiled in a very costly tax snafu. None of this made me nervous, however. My objective was to advance within the company and establish myself as a leader. The fact that the company had urgent problems gave me a greater opportunity to climb faster and establish myself sooner. (I always say you can't fall out of a basement.)

The company needed leaders to run their ailing units, so I got promoted rapidly and was soon running a components factory near Chicago. Running the factory taught me... well, how to run a factory. But the company, needing a quick cash infusion, decided to sell my factory.

Bad news for me?

Only if my ambition had ended with running one factory on the outskirts of Chicago. In fact, the company's plan to sell allowed me to do something I had never done before: execute a major-league deal to sell a business.

Fortunately, I was part of a very good selling team and learned the real art of the deal while I did the deal. It was like building the plane while flying it, but even this stunt is doable if you focus on process and procedure. The sale was successful, and, as it turned out, I could have remained with the factory under its new owner. But I didn't want that. I liked selling the business, and I wanted to sell more of them. So, I chose not to sell myself along with the factory, left the tech company, and was quickly hired by a maker of generating equipment, valued at $310 million at the time.

The company was looking to grow—the faster and farther, the better—through new products and acquisitions, and it wanted me because I had experience selling a business. I became part of a team that got the company into new and different channels, and, in this augmented incarnation, it was sold to a New York-based private equity firm for some $2 billion. The driver of its leap upward in value from $310 million was a natural disaster, Hurricane Katrina, which devastated the Gulf Coast in August 2005 and created a high demand for its products.

As the saying goes—or should go—one person's hurricane is another's windfall.

I now had the opportunity to go into private equity. But I wanted to be president of the sold company, and that would not happen in private equity. At this point, I decided I wanted to be a buyer and seller of businesses, but I realized I did not yet have nearly enough knowledge about running companies, and I wanted employment that would give me that knowledge. I knew sales and how to prepare a company to be sold. Now I needed to know how to actually run a company. This is when I moved to a major and quite diversified industrial, technical, and medical manufacturing conglomerate. It was not well known to the consumer public but was a big name in the business-to-business space.

Paramount among this conglomerate's management processes was the application of the 80/20 rule. If mathematics, as the old saying goes, is the queen of all sciences, 80/20 is the queen of all management processes. Also known as the Pareto principle, 80/20 has figured in every enterprise I have led. It may well be the single most important assumption in managing the processes of a business to achieve strategic growth. We will return to it repeatedly in this book, but let me offer a spoiler-in-a-box here.

Pareto's Enchanted Garden

Fig. 01-01: Vilfredo Pareto. *Credit: PD*

Among jacks-of-all-trades, Vilfredo Pareto (1848-1923) might be the jackiest of them all. He was a world-class civil engineer, sociologist, philosopher, political scientist, and economist. But what he loved most of all was gardening.

And because he loved it, he brought to it his other passions, especially the science of economics. When he observed that most of his healthy pea pods came from just a small number of his pea plants, he couldn't resist running the numbers. He found that roughly 80 percent of his healthy pods were produced by roughly just 20 percent of his pea plants. This 80/20 ratio stuck in his craw. He looked around him, *all* around him, and soon concluded that pretty much throughout the world, 80 percent of consequential results come from just 20 percent of causes.

Pareto discovered that 80/20 applied to nature. It was a fact of nature, like natural selection or the laws of thermodynamics. But the wild thing was that it also applied to sociological phenomena, political outcomes, economics—and, by extension, business and commerce. Give or take, it turned out to be a truly universal axiom.

He wrote about it, and so the Pareto principle was born. It's the idea that you can pretty much express any productive activity in terms of 80/20—the "trivial many" versus the "critical few." In business, this translates to 80 percent of revenue coming from just 20 percent of a company's customers. Likewise, 80 percent of revenue comes from just 20 percent of the company's products. Most importantly, 80 percent of revenue comes from the most productive 20 percent of your customers (call them your "A" customers), who buy 80 percent of your highest-performing products (the top 20 percent, your "A" products). What if you could devote 80 percent of your resources to serving just that 20 percent nexus of A customers buying A products?

Well, what's stopping you? Do it!

The Phoenix Instance

I learned to put 80/20 at the heart of all prioritization decisions. I have used it to guide strategy, strategic frameworks, and business plans in several companies throughout my career, and I will have a lot more to say about it in this book. Most recently, it has served me as the Jaws of Life to accelerate a good company that was wasting its potential.

Phoenix Industrial Technologies (real firm, fictitious name) is one of those companies with a low public profile but a great impact on its customers. A classic B2B enterprise, Phoenix is a distributor of mechanical components and engineering services, which means it is one of those meat-and-potatoes firms behind virtually anything that goes into making everything consumers buy and use. Phoenix has been around since the early 1960s, founded and operating mainly in the Midwest.

When it started, Phoenix distributed two categories of products: "power takeoffs" and air technologies. Power takeoffs are devices and components necessary to transmit mechanical power from one machine to another. Air technologies include air compressors and everything associated with them. The Air Technologies division also sold compressed air as a service to customers who did not want to invest in the capital expense of acquiring massive compressors. Phoenix would install equipment inside or outside a plant and supply air for a fixed contractual price.

After forty years, corporate leadership decided to sell Phoenix to a Chicago-based investment firm, which, after a few more years, sold it to a similar firm operating out of New York City. When it was sold the first time, Phoenix was under $100 million in size. It grew under the two prior sponsors, and by the time my firm acquired it, Phoenix was a true conglomerate, which included divisions that made devices for finishing materials, dispensing materials, motorizing things, managing fluid power, providing bearings on which devices spin, designing and building pumps of all kinds, and furnishing framing systems. To put it politely, Phoenix was diverse. To put it more accurately, more of a collection than an organization. Certainly, none of the previous acquirers had attempted to rationalize the organization. The systems, processes, and technologies were based on the original small company. But as many others joined the original small company in various locations, they did not talk to each other or operate in anything resembling a coordinated, let alone synergistic, fashion.

My firm recognized that the laissez-faire management style had worked well enough under former owners. It was, essentially, "We've bought you, and we'll leave you alone. Send us a check every quarter. If the check's big enough, we're going to be happy. If it's not, we're not going to be happy." My firm had no intention of following this strategy and planned to unlock the potential hidden deep inside the business.

At first, this hands-off management policy seemed to be working just fine. But management quickly noticed that what some would dismiss as a slump was shaping into a downward trend. Phoenix began experiencing falling sales, falling profit, and falling morale. The company I worked for recognized the need for an intervention. Phoenix was not run by "bad" or "inadequate" people, but its management did need directions and tools to enable it to start building more value quickly. Private equity is all about building value, and my company did not waste time before responding. They recognized that cutting, especially without a strategy, is hardly sufficient to build the value that turns a company around. We needed to act quickly. At the time, I thought of two classic lines from the master of lean dialog, Ernest Hemingway. They're from *The Sun Also Rises*:

"How did you go bankrupt?" Bill asked.
"Two ways," Mike said. "Gradually, then suddenly."

Well, at this point—somewhere between "gradually" and "suddenly"—the company took aggressive action to bend the curve upward. They put me on as Phoenix's new CEO with a single charge that boiled down to three words: *Fix Phoenix. Pronto.* It was an admirably concise order, which I translated into another three words: *create profitable growth.* And because it was urgent, I added a fourth: *Now!* The PE firm was excited and one-hundred-percent all-in with PGOS.

The PGOS at the core of this book is derived from my experience leading several companies. But Phoenix was special. It had dedicated people and the potential for greatness. The relentless cuts without a renewed strategy, however, had nudged it closer and closer to a breaking point. Scary though this was, it provided a unique opportunity to apply 80/20 and the other processes we will discuss. Growth was latent within this company, and it was my job to realize it, to turn potential energy into kinetic energy. The opportunity lay within the problem and the crisis. The threat was existential, and as Samuel Johnson, the eighteenth-century British literary critic, essayist, and lexicographer, put it, "Depend upon it, sir, when a man knows he is to be hanged in a fortnight, it concentrates his mind wonderfully."

I always preferred something a bit more cheerful: "You can't fall out of a basement." Follow the PGOS and let it guide you as you take strategic action to prioritize everything possible on the 20 percent of products and customers responsible for 80 percent of your revenue.

CHAPTER 2

Understand the Business

"In every institution, information is blood."

—BRADLEY H. PATTERSON, JR., The Ring of Power

BEFORE THOROUGHLY DIGGING into a business analytically, I usually ask straightforward questions about the business and its past, present, and future. There is nothing mystical about this. It's just a way to uncover what does not instantly meet the eye. You will find the complete list of my questions in chapter 6.

In his wonderful *Checklist Manifesto,* the American surgeon and writer Atul Gawande rates checklists as "among the basic tools of the quality and productivity... in virtually every field combining high risk and complexity. Checklists seem lowly and simplistic, but they help fill in for the gaps in our brains and between our brains." I learned a long time ago that having a checklist of questions saves you time and puts you into a mindset primed to pick up on relevant strengths and weaknesses. It may also help you confirm or refute any judgments you have already made. I, for one, came into the company with knowledge of one massive and obvious problem. Phoenix had succeeded for decades as a smallish ($90 million) company and was then sold to sponsor or private equity ownership, which agglomerated it into a $700 million-plus company. The rub? It was still being run with systems designed for the original $90 million company. The company's grossly underpowered processes were driving nothing more or less than chaos.

Grab Hold of the Stockdale Paradox

The late Admiral Jim Stockdale was the highest-ranking US military officer held as a POW during the Vietnam War. He was beaten and tortured some twenty times during his captivity from 1965 to 1973. He had no reason to believe he would live to see home and freedom again, but he nevertheless took command of his fellow POWs to lead them in a way that would exponentially increase their chances of survival.

Years after the war, *Good to Great* author Jim Collins had an opportunity to speak with Stockdale. He asked him how he got through his long ordeal alive and unbroken.

"I never doubted not only that I would get out," Stockdale told Collins, "but also that I would prevail in the end and turn the experience into the defining event of my life, which, in retrospect, I would not trade."

Rendered all but speechless by Stockdale's response, Collins asked, "Who didn't make it out?"

"Oh, that's easy. The optimists."

Naturally, Collins was puzzled, but Stockdale explained that the optimists "were the ones who said, 'We're going to be out by Christmas.' And Christmas would come, and Christmas would go. Then they'd say, 'We're going to be out by Easter.' And Easter would come, and Easter would go. And then Thanksgiving, and then it would be Christmas again. And they died of a broken heart."

The lesson Stockdale took from this is that you must never lose your confidence that you will ultimately prevail, but you must never let this belief cause you to abandon the "discipline to confront the most brutal facts of your current reality, whatever they might be." Today, this is called the Stockdale Paradox.

How do you remain disciplined?

Through *process.*

Stockdale gave his fellow prisoners processes for prevailing, getting through torture, secretly communicating with one another, and other procedures and routines.

If process can mean the difference between rational hope and darkest despair—if it can mean the difference between living and dying under the worst conditions imaginable—it can certainly guide you to success in managing even the most challenging business situations.

I asked the questions about past performance and discovered there had been no growth before 2016, when one of the former private equity firms bought it. Up to that time, every company added to Phoenix performed worse than at the time of acquisition. I dug deeper into this and found a story that clarified the problem and pointed to a solution. You must always assume that the answers are out there. Ask the right people. If you don't know who the right people are, ask whomever you can. Even if they may be the wrong people, they should be able to suggest somebody with the answers. The failure to get answers usually begins with a failure to ask questions. Obvious—but no less true.

Ponder the Answers and Make Decisions

Hands-off though they wanted to be, my employer was a supremely diligent steward of its companies. It wanted to know why the performance of the acquisition declined once the company had been acquired. Management set out to get the answer and discovered it was twofold. First, the previous owner of Phoenix had been functioning as an absentee CEO, spending most of his time away from the company. Second, there was no discernable growth strategy during their tenure—well, no strategy except acquisition, which can be more of a reflex than a strategy. Armed with this answer, the firm acted on it, moving the previous owner out of the CEO role.

The search for a new CEO began, during which, some eighteen months, the Phoenix company experienced the full force of the pandemic, shut down a bunch of facilities, laid off many people, and started combining assets. When I discovered this, I had the answer to several questions I always ask when I come in to lead a company. The attempt to restore growth by reducing costs through non-strategically shedding assets, including human capital, is a common response to decline. However, when done strategically, cuts, like skillful surgery, can be lifesaving and even life-restoring. When cuts are made across the board, willy-nilly, I have never known them to work, and wherever I see this behavior, I know that I am staring at a bright red flag. A company attempting to cut its way to profitability only gets into deeper trouble as management is hollowed out.

A Chainsaw Is Not an Instrument of Strategy

There *is* such a thing as a strategic layoff. But when layoffs become a mere reflex, there is no strategy. It is a response aimed at outlays without regard to revenue. You cannot save the village by destroying it.

You might conclude that when I was finally brought on as Phoenix's CEO in 2021, I didn't need to do much evaluation. Most of the causes of damage were in plain sight. But the truth is that when something is bad enough to look obviously wrong, what you are *not* seeing in plain sight is usually even worse.

This, that, and this are wrong. So, stop doing this, that, and this. They were all obvious problems that seemed—to me, at least—eminently fixable. Besides, one of the factors that motivated me to take the job was my familiarity with many of the distributors that amalgamated into Phoenix. So, I figured that, underneath all the mess, we had great products, exclusivity in key territories, and a lot of good people on our team. This makes for a strong reoccurring revenue stream. In other words, the fundamentals were there. There was nothing wrong with Phoenix that couldn't be fixed.

"I think I can turn it around," I said aloud.

The truth is that I didn't realize just how much trouble Phoenix was in when I accepted the role of CEO. Maybe that was because so many problems were so evident that I stopped looking for more, including more sources of difficulty. At the same time, I had not recognized all the opportunities. It's not that the obvious answers are wrong; it's just that they may not be the only answers.

You Don't Need a Microscope, but You Do Need to Get on the Ground

I was named CEO of Phoenix on August 9, 2021. My first and immediate objective was to *understand the business* thoroughly. To do this, I had to

1. Identify obvious and pressing problems and fix them.
2. Analyze the business.
3. Understand the current strategy and modify it to align with business objectives.

Steps 1 and 2 can be most effectively launched by asking the questions I posed at the beginning of this chapter, but never let the analysis get in the way of immediately addressing the most obvious, urgent, and existential problems. "Existential problems" are those that threaten imminent harm. Almost always, these are issues of revenue. Do first what you must do to stay in business and buy time to fix everything else. If you let the business die, you have nothing left to fix.

Existential Problems, Existential Solutions

If your house is on fire, put out the fire.
If your boat has a leak, patch the hole.

Take a Three L Tour and Beyond

You don't need to start with a microscope. In fact, you may never need such an instrument. What is required is an understanding of the business from a ground perspective. When I arrived at Phoenix, I went on a "Three L Tour": listening, learning, and leveraging. I just went out and started talking to everybody. My first questions are always variations of "What's happening?" They boil down to "How's the business? What's working? What's not working? Tell me what you like about your job and what you don't. What's going right and wrong?"

I find it very helpful to moderate the spontaneity of a Three L Tour by circulating in advance a simple list of questions to help people think about what they want to say. With key managers in the organization, I take an even more programmed approach by setting up a series of three one-on-one meetings, which are only slightly more formal versions of the Three L Tour. The first meeting could be titled "Getting Acquainted." In advance, I send my counterpart in the scheduled interview an easygoing, informal questionnaire:

Meeting 1: Getting Acquainted
Getting to know each other on a personal level
Things I Would like to Know:

1. Tell me about your work and your role. What skills do you bring to your role?
2. What are the most rewarding aspects of your job?
3. Why do you do your job (besides for the paycheck)?
4. How can I support you?
5. What brings out the best in you? What are your work preferences and styles?
6. How would you describe the business and what's working or not working?
7. What are you most proud of in this past year? Why?
8. What do you like to do when you're not working?
9. If you could make a request to anyone in the company, what would you ask for? Why?

Potential Topics You Might like to Share:

1. What I would like Bill to know about me is...
2. I would describe my own leadership style as...
3. What excites me most about my role is...
4. My single greatest concern is...
5. The two things that would help us be more successful are...
6. To get the most out of my performance, it helps to...
7. What requires our immediate attention is...
8. I consider your (Bill's) top three priorities to be...

I take time to digest the first meeting—in other words, to really get acquainted. When I feel ready, I set up the second set of one-on-one meetings, which are devoted to *discussing the business*.

Meeting 2: Discussing the Business
Let's talk about the business and your role.

Topics That Will Help Me Learn How the Organization Works:

1. Business performance—objectives, goals, strategies, tactics, financials.
2. People and team—how are things working in your area? How do we engage our people? Who are our high performers? What is the level of engagement?
3. Customers—what do customers say about our products? What challenges are we facing in the market?
4. Distributors, vendors, and partnerships—what is our strategy for working with others? Who are considered our strategic partners?
5. Processes—how are the processes enabling or hindering work outputs?
6. Working across the organization—how do you and your team work with other areas?
7. Opportunities and challenges—provide examples.
8. Support—what support do you need from me, and what other resource requirements do you have?
9. Professional career development—what are your career aspirations?
10. Miscellaneous—what other advice do you have as we move forward?

Again, I take the time to study my notes from this meeting before setting up the third round, which is a *deeper dive business review*.

Meeting 3: Deeper Dive Business Review
Opportunity to validate and confirm knowledge about the business and to seek input on next steps

Deeper Dive from Second Meeting as Well as the Following:

1. Continued discussion of the business and topics raised in meeting 2
2. Key initiatives in which you are involved
3. Opportunities and challenges for all parties
4. Risks the company faces
5. Resource requirements
6. Process or system requirements
7. Talent review of your team

Focus on What Is Important, Both the Urgent and the Nonurgent—Avoid Everything Else

Based on your Three L Tour and meetings with key managers, you are ready to analyze the business. Just don't get too comfortable about it. Your tour and meetings should be sufficient to alert you to issues of obvious urgency.

If your house is on fire, put out the fire. If your boat is leaking, patch the holes. Address the existential problems. Develop a bias for action. If something obvious needs fixing, fix it. You can always fine-tune later; if your initial fix is ineffective, try something else. An effective leader learns how to identify high-priority problems quickly and then focus efforts on them. With obvious problems, your objective should be to make a major impact swiftly.

Identify your A-item priorities. Get early wins on these, and you will not only address existential problems that threaten the business in the short term, but the early wins you gain will lift morale throughout the organization and inspire confidence in your leadership as well as in what psychologists call the "self-efficacy" of the company's people—their belief that they possess the knowledge, skill, and competence to solve their problems, leverage their opportunities, and perform their assigned missions. These early wins and self-efficacy attitudes are critical to building valuable momentum to drive the organization to accomplish all strategic goals.

A-item priorities bear the following hallmarks:

1. They flow from fundamental problems.
2. They are specific rather than vague or general.
3. They suggest a clear direction but also allow for flexibility so that actions can be modified to suit a changing situation or fresh information and data about the current and evolving situation.

When the Japanese attack on Pearl Harbor thrust the United States into World War II on December 7, 1941, US Army Chief of Staff General George C. Marshall summoned Brigadier General Dwight D. Eisenhower to Washington, DC. There, Marshall quickly summed up the catastrophic situation in the Pacific: the fleet at Pearl Harbor had been smashed, Wake Island was under heavy attack, Guam had fallen, the possessions of US Allies Britain and the Netherlands had fallen or were about to fall, and the Philippines, at the time a US commonwealth territory, was about to be invaded. It was a litany of disaster, and Marshall had one question for Eisenhower: "What should be our general course of action?"

Ike knew there was no feasible fix, but he asked Marshall for a few hours to formulate a reply and returned later that day to lay out what he considered the only immediately viable course: do everything militarily possible, no matter how little, by establishing a base of operations in Australia. "The people of China, of the Philippines, of the Dutch East Indies will be watching us. They may excuse failure, but they will not excuse abandonment." This was *not* a formula for quick victory. Why not? Because quick victory was impossible in this situation. Yet it was the first step in a process of ultimate victory.

Marshall agreed with Ike's proposal and recognized Eisenhower as a leader willing and able to provide realistic and productive responses even to hopeless situations. What was needed at the moment was an alternative to surrender. In other words, what was needed was a first step away from surrender. Marshall understood this and immediately named Eisenhower, hitherto an obscure officer, assistant chief of the Army War Plans Division. He was promoted to major general. In a short time, Eisenhower would become the supreme Allied commander in Europe. He would run the war against Germany and its Allies.

In his answer to Marshall, Eisenhower put into practice a prioritizing framework he explained years later, in 1954, when he was president of the United States: "I have two kinds of problems," President Eisenhower said, "the urgent and the important. The urgent are not important, and the important are never urgent." Famed business thinker and author Steven Covey borrowed Eisenhower's thought process and devised the following action matrix:

Urgent	Not Urgent
I **(Manage)** • Crisis • Medical emergencies • Pressing problems • Deadline-driven projects • Last-minute preparations for scheduled activities **Quadrant of Necessity**	**II** **(Focus)** • Preparation/planning • Prevention • Values clarification • Exercise • Relationship-building • True recreation/relaxation **Quadrant of Quality & Personal Leadership**
III **(Avoid)** • Interruptions, some calls • Some mail & reports • Some meetings • Many "pressing" matters • Many popular activities **Quadrant of Deception**	**IV** **(Avoid)** • Trivia, busywork • Junk mail • Some phone messages/ email • Time wasters • Escape activities • Viewing mindless TV show **Quadrant of Waste**

(Left margin labels: Important / Not Important)

Fig. 02-01.

This matrix will help you to execute a key principle: *focus on what is important, both the urgent and the nonurgent. Avoid everything else.* The fact is that urgent problems demand attention because the consequences of not addressing them are usually serious and immediate. Yet urgent problems are almost always imposed on you. They embody somebody else's goals, whereas important issues are key to achieving your goals—your strategic ends—even though their consequences might be less immediate.

Begin by distinguishing the important from the unimportant. Set the unimportant aside. The urgent and nonurgent are important, but for practical, existential reasons, you must address the urgent first—without forsaking the nonurgent for long. If you know what is important *and* urgent, you can focus on these issues while reserving enough time to focus on the nonurgent.

CHAPTER 3

Purpose, Strategy, Execution

◆ ◆ ◆

"It almost looks as if analysis were the third of those 'impossible' professions in which one can be quite sure of unsatisfying results. The other two... are the bringing up of children and the government of nations."

—SIGMUND FREUD

NOW THAT YOU understand the business, you are positioned to analyze the business. This begins with more questions; this time, however, you ask them not of others but of yourself.

Analyze the business! The French mechanical, mathematical, and scientific genius Pierre Simon Laplace (1749-1827) invented statistical analysis (for all intents and purposes). Above all else, he believed that true analysis would require "an intelligence which could comprehend all the forces by which nature is animated and the respective positions of the beings which compose it." Any thorough analysis would require a formula that applies to "the movements of the largest bodies in the universe and those of the lightest atom" so that "nothing would be uncertain, and the future as the past would be present" in that formula.

Well, I'm no polymath, I don't command the level of all-knowing intelligence Laplace recommends, and I don't possess the formula he posits. Most of all, *I don't have the time!* But, as a CEO, I know I can make a good beginning in analyzing any business by asking pertinent questions about its past performance as compared to its present performance. And while the present moment requires initial focus on the urgent, focusing without undue delay on the future allows me to consider the nonurgent but important issues that will allow the company to realize its major goals.

Define Success

Google this phrase: "The unaimed arrow never misses." You will find many references but little enlightenment beyond the hope that remaining open to serendipity may lead you to great experiences and unforeseen inspiration. Granted, the unaimed arrow approach holds some promise for living your life. But it is just plain bad for business. Business needs targets. Your enterprise can neither fail nor succeed in reaching goals that do not exist. In other words, if you don't aim the arrow, you will not miss, but why even launch it?

- Defining **success** must produce an understanding of your **purpose.**
- Understanding your **purpose** must guide **intention** in everything everybody in the company (especially the managing executives) says and does.
- Only after **success**, **purpose**, and **intention** are defined can a meaningful strategy be built.
- To be **successful**, that **strategy**, whatever it is, must contain the means of its **execution**.
- That is, **execution** is integral to a successful **strategy**. It follows that failed **execution** is failed **strategy.**

Unless the company's leadership defines success before building a strategy and the processes necessary to execute it, the company will be an unaimed arrow. "Success" cannot be left as a vague concept—a feeling. In business, success must be visualized and quantified. This makes it a bull's-eye painted on a target. As fabulist Aesop said, "A sensible man never embarks on an enterprise until he can see his way clear to the end of it."

People have many motives for starting a business, but a primary motive is almost always to make money. The iconic oracle of management, Peter Drucker, proclaimed that the "purpose of business is to create a customer." *Investopedia* defines a "customer" as "an individual or business that purchases another company's good or services." So, the customer is the source of money. In business, money is measured in profit and loss, revenue versus margin, ROI, and competitive ranking—all objectively based metrics, which are a durable paint for drawing a bull's-eye.

It does not follow, however, that leading a company to success requires nothing more than setting clear financial goals and practicing good accounting. In 1994, Jim Collins and Jerry I. Porras published *Built to Last: Successful Habits of Visionary Companies*. They defined "visionary companies" as the "premier institutions—the crown jewels—in their industries, widely admired by their peers and having a long track record of making significant impact on the world around them." Such firms are built to last because they are visionary companies.

The word "visionary" has vague and even gauzy connotations. For me, leaders who can create built-to-last strategy are visionary in that they can visualize success and the associated goals for themselves and others. They can paint a picture of success *and* show others in the company where they fit into that picture. Here's an example of this. On August 12, 1877, Thomas Edison drew a rough but clear sketch of a machine he envisioned. He wrote in the lower left-hand corner of the paper an instruction to his senior machinist, John Kruesi, to "Make this," and he placed it on Kruesi's workbench. He made no further explanation. He did not have to. As Edison knew his superb craftsman would, Kruesi made it, and the phonograph—along with the unprecedented phenomenon of *recorded* sound—entered the world.

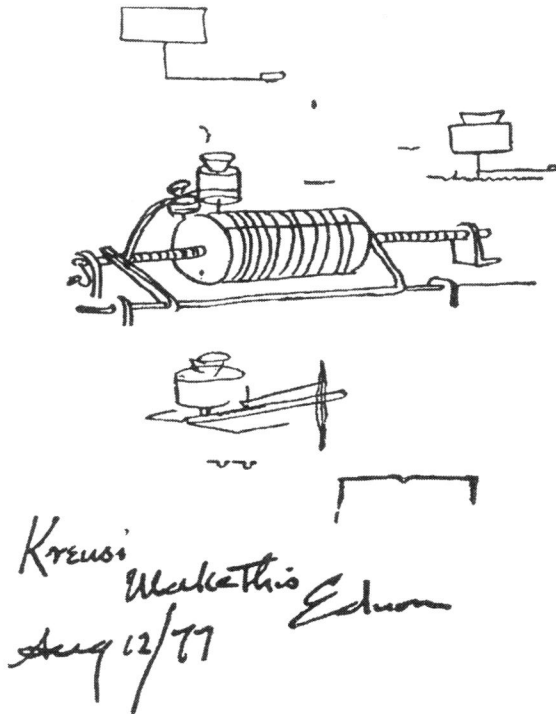

Fig. 03-01: Edison's working drawing for the phonograph.
Credit: Science History Images/Alamy Stock Photo

Thomas Edison was my kind of visionary. He was a leader capable of showing others—not with gauzy imagery but with pragmatic precision—what success looks like. He sketched the future, or, more precisely, *a* future *he* defined as possessing technology capable of recording and playing back sound, which had never been done before. For any individual or organization, "success" is an aspiration, a vision of some desired future state, until it is achieved and thus becomes a success. For a business built to last, "success" is the repeated outcome of many, many successful cycles of strategic execution. As David J. Mahoney, president of Good Humor and Canada Dry, said, "Success is not so much achievement as achieving." He advised aspiring executives to refuse "to join the cautious crowd that plays not to lose; play to win."

I don't know if John Kruesi was "inspired" by Edison's drawing. But he built what Edison asked him to build, and I am certain that the result inspired him. After he presented the assembled device to Edison, the inventor spoke into it while turning the crank on a cylinder wrapped in foil. He stopped, returned the stylus and diaphragm assembly to its starting position, and turned the crank again, and his own *recorded* voice came out of the machine. He had "visualized" the future state to which he aspired, Kruesi built it, and the aspiration became reality. There was no high-flown rhetoric, no cheerleading of any kind. All he offered was a clear vision. And that was quite enough.

In *The Inspiring Leader: Unlocking the Secrets of How Extraordinary Leaders Motivate,* authors John H. Zenger, Joseph R. Folkman, and Scott Edinger ask, "What makes an outstanding leader?" Based on extensive research—a database of more than 200,000 multi-rater or 360-degree feedback instruments that described 20,000 managers—they concluded that a single leadership quality emerged as more important than any other. It was the ability to inspire and motivate high performance. The key to such inspiration was the ability to present a compelling vision of the company's future state and to do so in a way that is as pragmatically clear as Edison's line drawing.

Let me boil that down for you. Inspiring leadership shows others what success looks like. If you can show how each person on the team fits into the picture, you stand a good chance of inspiring the actions, behaviors, and performances capable of transforming the picture into reality.

A truly inspiring visionary knows what should be embodied in the company's strategy and knows that it must be capable of being presented clearly and concisely. Employees will never become a team without such clarity—the clarity of a sharp line drawing. They may work hard, but they will be pulling and pushing in every which way. They will be unable to execute a strategy they do not fully understand. They will be a quiver of so many unaimed arrows.

Defining the target that is success requires articulating purpose, strategy, and execution in ways that are as concrete as the vision Edison was able to present to his talented employee. It is necessary that everyone at every level of the enterprise understands the mission, vision, and values of the company and shares this same understanding.

Volumes have been written about mission, vision, and values. I will offer an example of the mission, vision, and values of Phoenix, the company I was brought in to lead.

MISSION

Phoenix Industrial Technologies improves manufacturing operations through our breadth of product, best-in-class technical and engineering knowledge, and superior customer service to lead in every market in which we choose to do business.

VISION

A reenvisioned industry where Phoenix Industrial Technologies provides turnkey solutions that improve uptime, labor safety, and energy conservation on a broad scale, improving the world around us.

VALUES

Integrity:

We will do what we say we will do. Our words and actions will be honest, ethical, and respectful.

Achievement:

We pride ourselves on achieving our goals and being judged in our work for our individual and collective accomplishments.

Expertise:

We provide tailored, expert solutions for various industries and work hard to provide you with the right solution beyond other industrial distributors.

Partnership:

We are a true long-term partner dedicated to providing solutions that improve day-to-day operations.

Investment:

We are proud to be committed to investing in our people and innovative technology with an eye focused on the future.

Balance:

We empower our teams to enjoy life, work passionately, play hard, and appreciate what life offers.

Divergent and Convergent Thinking

While everyone in the enterprise must understand and buy into the company's mission, vision, and values, something even more basic must be shared to create success through processes capable of formulating a purpose, building a strategy, and efficiently executing it. This "something" is thought itself. Before getting too excited about it, consider Ralph Waldo Emerson's question and answer: "What is the hardest task in the world? To think."

We can make it a little easier. Guided by the principles covered in part I, the processes in chapter 4 and parts II and III are divided into two distinct cognitive approaches. This makes thinking a little less daunting than it appeared to Emerson. Let me explain.

Psychologists and HR professionals often speak of divergent and convergent thinking. The two terms were first proposed in 1956 by psychologist J. P. Guilford, who observed that, faced with a problem to solve, some people tend to brainstorm, generating multiple ideas, several solutions, and an array of alternatives. Others, however, tend to focus immediately on finding a single solution to the problem at hand and then drill down to define it fully. Guilford and others who have followed up on this divergent/convergent distinction argued that divergent thinkers were more "creative" than convergent thinkers, who were guided more by logic than creative imagination. In the world of HR, the classic Myers-Briggs personality test, which is still often used to evaluate job applicants, looked to discover whether a candidate or an employee was a "thinker"—a person who made generally objective decisions based on analysis of facts or data—versus a "feeler," who was guided more by subjective feelings and gut instincts. Thinkers are logical, while feelers are creative.

Now, there is value and truth in the distinction between divergent and convergent thinking and in recognizing that some people lean more toward a divergent approach to problem-solving while others favor a convergent approach. We come into the workplace with certain aptitudes, traits, tendencies, biases, and mindsets, some pushing us into the divergent camp versus the convergent camp. Let's grant this.

Let's also acknowledge that some managers and executives value divergent thinkers more, while others want convergent thinkers. Many high-level executives claim to want—and are willing to reward—people who "think outside the box." Divergent thinkers, they believe (or say they believe), are the ones who give an organization an innovative edge over the competition. They create products and services that are differentiating. They possess faculties embodying a kind of genius or even magic. They are the rainmakers. Some thought leaders classify divergent thinkers as creative "insurgents" versus the stale "incumbents," who have been in charge seemingly forever and are more concerned with protecting the status quo than risking innovation.

The iconic example of the insurgent divergent thinker is Steve Jobs, cofounder of Apple, a company whose longtime motto was "Think Different." Famously, Jobs took the development of his early pet project, the Macintosh (Mac) computer, not only out of the mainstream Apple corporate bureaucracy but out of the Apple headquarters building itself. He put the "Mac group" together in a rented building located in a strip mall across the street from the original Apple campus, hoisted a Jolly Roger pirate flag over the building, and let them do their divergent thing out of the grasp of the corporate hierarchy, out of the main corporate building, and out of the box.

This vision of Steve Jobs ignores that the cofounder of Apple was Stephen Gary Wozniak. Woz was the guy who operationalized much of Jobs's vision. Woz was certainly—indeed, by definition—an innovator but, compared to Jobs, was more convergent than divergent. It's not that he couldn't or didn't think outside the box, but that his thinking built *new* boxes. Literally. He knew how to build, solder, and write code. The first "boxes" he built were the Apple I (more a circuit board than a box) and the Apple II.

The truth is that successful businesses combine divergent and convergent thinking. We may talk a lot about, praise, value, and even revere those who think outside the box, but as Tim Nelson and Jim McGee recognized in their 2013 book *Think Inside the Box: Discover the Exceptional Business Inside Your Organization*, convergent thinkers are as essential as divergent ones.

The lesson Jobs and Woz and a book that dares to laud the virtues of thinking *inside* the box teach is that we all need to get beyond typecasting, evaluating, and valuing people based on whether they *are* or *are not* divergent or convergent thinkers. Leading, managing, and doing business involves both divergent and convergent thinking. Some phases of business require one to the exclusion of the other or one in preference to the other, while other phases require divergent and convergent thinking simultaneously. It stands to reason, then, that we should get comfortable with both styles of thought. Climb outside the box when the time or circumstances call for it, but get right back inside when time and circumstance call for that.

Don't Use a Hammer When You Need a Screwdriver

We should stop defining divergent and convergent thinking as traits, talents, or habits. They are tools to be used when needed. As with any set of tools, you do have to know which ones to use when and where.

You see before you two pieces of wood and some screws. Your assignment is to join the two pieces together. Which of the following do you do?

    A.   Get a screwdriver and screw the pieces together
    B.   Get a hammer and pound the pieces together

You choose A. You may understand that B is possible. You can probably pound a screw into the wood like a nail. The results won't be pretty, and almost certainly, the assembly will not be as strong as if you had used the proper tool. So, you choose A.

You choose it not because a screwdriver is inherently better than a hammer but because it is the better tool for the fastener and material. You also choose the screwdriver not because you are better at handling a screwdriver than wielding a hammer but because it is the appropriate tool for the fastener and material you are working with.

Of course, there is another possible choice. On the theory that if using one tool is good, using two is better, you could screw the screw in part way and then hammer it home. Or you could hammer it part way and then finish the job with a screwdriver. However, the fact is that combining these two tools simply requires more effort and does not result in a better bond.

Now, back to the other two tools—divergent and convergent thinking. In most business organizations, there is a belief that success results from differentiation in the marketplace. This requires combining innovation and an entrepreneurial mindset with objective evaluation and the ability to execute and evaluate. Yet simply combining these two contrasting approaches is not the optimal way of bringing both into the conduct of the business.

Divergent thinking is about imagining a wide range of possibilities. It is about suspending skepticism and disbelief for a time to play out the broadest possible range of scenarios. It is about asking, "What if..." It gives free rein to an urge to head off in unconventional directions. Instead of going out to round up the usual suspects, you deliberately look for the unusual suspects. Divergent thinking is a laboratory for thought experiments. Everything is on the table. As Steve Jobs would have said, divergent thinking is about "thinking different."

Divergent thinking is the funnel turned upside down. The thought process runs from the narrow end and spreads through the wide end. Convergent thinking, in contrast, uses the funnel in its conventional configuration, the wide part narrowing into a tube. Convergent thinking is not about multiplying options but narrowing them. If you have started with ten choices, convergent thinkers want to reduce them to three or two or, best of all, just one. It is possible to apply imagination in this narrowing process, just as it is possible to hammer a screw. It is possible but not very effective. The optimal approach in convergent thinking is driven less by imagination and feeling than by data gathering, analysis of that data, logical reasoning, logical argument, and criticism to tease out the best options while culling out the least satisfactory ones. There is always the danger that some promising alternatives will be jettisoned. But this may be preferable to chasing wild rabbits down some very deep and twisting rabbit holes.

Why not just approach everything with a mixture of divergent and convergent thinking? While the combination may produce some interesting arguments, the greater likelihood is that the two extremes will simply cancel one another out. The convergent thinking will tend to suffocate the divergent thinking, while the divergent thinking will muddy the clarity of the highly focused convergent thinking. Still, your business decisions benefit from both divergent and convergent thinking. To keep them from stepping on one another, however, you need to follow a process that uses them sequentially, where each is most powerful, rather than simultaneously, where the one cancels out the other.

Brainstorm First, Meet Second

Call a meeting, and you will likely get an avalanche of convergent thinking. The atmosphere of most business meetings is analytical and critical. This is because most meetings cast most attendees in the role of auditors. They are there to examine and criticize.

Don't fight this natural drift toward convergent thinking. Instead, assemble the right gathering for the right purpose. If you are planning the coming year's business concentration, for example, you want to ensure that there is room for divergent and convergent thinking. Planning begins with a situation assessment of the business as it currently exists. This starts by gathering data and performing a business analysis of it in terms of current customers, portfolios, markets, and competitors.

Up to this point, the approach is mostly convergent—dominated by analysis and objective reasoning. Assuming that your organization is committed to growth and not the maintenance of the status quo, you need to decide at what point you want the people in the organization to start "thinking different." If the time has come now, don't call another meeting. Instead, convene a brainstorming session or a series of them.

If you want tomorrow to be different from today, do something different today. Don't meet. Brainstorm. At most meetings, you would not encourage anyone to go out of their way to develop an outlandish idea. However, at the brainstorming session's pivot point, that is exactly what you want to encourage. Get people out of the box. Encourage divergence by asking for ideas, emphasizing inclusion and quantity. Discourage censorship—self-censorship and censorship of or by others.

The ancient Greeks worshipped *both* Dionysius and Apollo. The one embodied human nature's spontaneous, sensual, emotional, and even wild aspects. The other emphasized the rational, self-disciplined, orderly dimensions of human nature. In encouraging the generation of new ideas, unleash the Dionysian impulses. Expand the possible. Nurture intuition, gut feeling, emotion, impulse, and freewheeling imagination. Call for discovery of possibilities and opportunities. Multiply available options to expand the playing field. Drive the brainstorming session to encourage speed, surprise, and playfulness. Emphasize the novel and the untried. Encourage curiosity. Ask *what if?* Propose something wild and challenging. Then harvest as many responses as you can get.

In the phase of divergent thinking, you want to bring to the surface ways to serve current customers better, to sell them new products and services, to make them want to choose you, and to recognize ways in which current customers are changing and how you can change to retain them and serve them better. You want to consider changing your current portfolio by imagining a future portfolio. You want to consider expanding current markets, getting out of certain markets, and creating new markets with new customers. You want to examine new alternatives to gain a decisive competitive advantage. The emphasis in divergent thinking is on *more*—more options, more possibilities, more opportunities, more risk.

Some people find divergent thinking fun, exhilarating, and playful. Others find it scary, upsetting, and generally off-putting. Nevertheless, it should generate a surplus of ideas. Many of them will be questionable, unworkable, or just plain bad. That's fine. Decisions are not finalized at the high-flying altitude of the divergent thinking phase. Once you have gathered an array of issues, opportunities, and possible directions for the business going forward, and once you and your organization have done some reimagining of the business in a global context and from the perspective of *anything is possible*, it is time for the diastole of divergence to enter the systole of convergence. The Apollonian perspective needs to take charge of the Dionysian impulse, and the playing field needs to be narrowed as the focus sharpens from what is possible to what is executable. From creating endless choices, the meetings (for they are now meetings rather than brainstorming sessions) focus on making choices. The pace of the meetings becomes slower and is characterized less by exhilaration than deliberation. Playfulness yields to analysis, sequencing, sorting, measuring, testing, and creating solutions. Where the work of divergent thought tends toward the qualitative, that of convergent thinking is quantitative. Imagination yields hard-edged realism, and freewheeling invention gives way to structure. The fuel of divergent thought is inclusion. Convergence applies the brakes in the form of filtering and exclusion. Instead of judgment by subjective measures—feelings, gut responses—objective indexes are sought and applied. The realm of divergence is an empire of ideas. The space in which convergent thinking operates is action. Whereas the work products of divergent thinking are chiefly discovery and definition, those of convergence are development and delivery. During the brainstorming of divergence, a single question or provocation was intended to produce a bumper crop of responses. In contrast, convergent thought aspires to arrive at a single unified response from the entire organization. Businesses call this alignment.

While navigating the expanding universe of divergent thinking, the underlying focus is on all the issues and opportunities facing the business in the coming year or other periods. During the phase in which the tool of convergent thinking dominates, it is the potential implications of those issues and opportunities that are explored. This provides the insight necessary to prioritize those issues and opportunities, reducing them to something that is manageable in a literal business sense.

As wonderful as the phase of divergent thought can be, it is in the convergent thinking phase that ideas are chosen, narrowed, culled, and then transformed into a framework for execution before new policies, approaches, and products can arise.

CHAPTER 4

It's the Trivial Many Versus the Critical Few

"Whenever you see a successful business, someone once made a courageous decision."

—PETER F. DRUCKER

LET'S AGREE THAT, in business, it's important to do important things. Conversely, it's not just unimportant to do unimportant things, it is downright destructive because it squanders work, time, people, and other assets that should be devoted to doing important things. These two propositions are valuable because they take you directly to steps 1 and 2 in making just about any business decision.

> Step 1: Decide what is important. Decide what is unimportant.
> Step 2: Do what is important. Avoid what is unimportant.

Simple, yes? Now, you only need to know how to decide what is important and what is not. Some aspects of this decision are complex, requiring judgment based on experience, expertise, awareness of relevant technology, innovation, trends, price points, price sensitivities, etc. Factors such as these require market research and deliberative thought. Yet there is a key element in this decision that is strikingly straightforward. It begins with pea plants and peapods.

The Lesson of the Pea

In chapter 1, we mentioned Vilfredo Pareto. Born in Paris in 1848, he was what we call a polymath. Everything interested him. His professional life began as a civil engineer, but he also made important contributions to sociology, political science, economics, and philosophy. He always found time for another great passion: gardening. Even polymaths need an escape from the daily grind. But for Pareto, there was no escaping the analytical side of his brain. As he puttered, he couldn't help calculating that just 20 percent of the pea plants in his garden produced 80 percent of his healthy pea pods. Through patient observation, he determined that this wasn't a fluke but a general truth, and this realization produced his personal eureka moment.

He applied his observation of peas in his back garden to "uneven distribution" in a vast array of fields. From pea plants, he turned to the distribution of wealth in Italy (though born in Paris, his family was Genoese, and he spent most of his working life in Italy). He determined that 80 percent of the nation's land was owned by just 20 percent of the population. He then turned to the characteristics of industrial production. His calculations revealed that 80 percent of industrial output came from just 20 percent of industrial companies. Ultimately, he applied the 80/20 lens to just about every measurably productive human activity and concluded that in any such endeavor, 80 percent of the results come from just 20 percent of the action.

This is the Pareto principle, often called the 80/20 rule or principle. If you are more expansive, you can also refer to it as the law of the vital few. If you prefer an even more hard-nosed outlook, you can say that 80/20 separates the "critical few" from the "trivial many." However you put it, the Pareto principle asserts that a minority of actions, causes, or inputs produces the majority of results, outputs, or rewards. More important for business, the Pareto principle allows us to translate the words "majority" and "minority" into a rough ratio: 80/20.

Just how dramatic is this insight?

Well, begin by applying it to yourself. Measured by the Pareto principle, 80 percent of what you achieve in your job comes from 20 percent of the time you spend working at it. Put another way, 80 percent of what you do—four-fifths of your effort—is essentially irrelevant.

Ouch!

Maybe it will make you feel better when I explain that by "you," I mean "one," "we," or "everybody." For you are not alone. We are all in the same boat. You may find that hard to believe because it contradicts what we expect of ourselves or any reasonably competent worker. But the Pareto principle should not be taken as a personal criticism. It is based on observation. In everything from the growth of pea plants to the work of laborers, craftsmen, and professionals, there is a built-in imbalance between causes and results, inputs and outputs, efforts and rewards. The 80/20 principle applies to work, markets, customers, products— virtually every aspect of business. Rather than try to evade or deny it, embrace it, use it, and leverage it to optimize performance and increase your company's competitive edge.

Move from Measurement to Improvement

Executives, managers, and the rank and file often complain about the profusion of reports that cascade through their organization. Maybe there *are* too many reports. For example, Erwin Knoll, who wrote for the *Washington Post* in the 1960s and edited *The Progressive,* an influential magazine and website covering politics and culture, once noted that the New York Department of Mental Hygiene "produced and distributed a three-page illustrated memorandum on how to split an English muffin." But in my experience, the problem is not a superabundance of reports about trivial matters but a plethora of reports that consist of mere measurements. A truly useful report begins with *measurement*, of course, but concludes by applying measurement to *improvement*. If more reports that routinely circulate through our businesses were dedicated to achieving improvement rather than simply measuring current conditions and leaving it there, no one would complain about too many reports.

The 80/20 principle is based on measurement and intended as a statement of general fact. It is up to executives and managers to take the principle from observation to application, from measurement to improvement. I know it's hard (Ralph Waldo Emerson said so!), but thinking is required. If you want tomorrow to be different from today, do something different today. Use 80/20 to show you what to do "different."

Begin by applying 80/20 to every aspect of the business—to customers, markets, products, and processes. The purpose is not to observe and call it a day but to identify the truly critical—the vital—and devote your resources to those opportunities. Instead of continuing to input 80 percent to get 20 percent—taking resources from what is vital and squandering them on what is irrelevant—improve performance by segmenting your customers and products to ensure that your organization devotes the lion's share of its resources to products and customers that are most productive.

Create Quartiles

Segmenting customers and products starts with the first foundational tool of 80/20, called a quartile. Quartiles set up the second, more powerful tool, called a quadrant or "quad."

For both products and customers, start with one year of sales (shipments) data. Be sure to include the product (and any important product details), customer (and any important customer details), sales, quantity, cost of the materials used (cost of goods sold will do if material cost is unavailable), and the resulting profit margin.

1. Force-rank your *products* by sales/revenue/turnover.
2. Divide the products into four equally sized quartiles (e.g., if you have 1,000 products, each quartile contains 250 products).
3. Summarize each quartile by total revenue, percent of total revenue, margin, percent of margin, maximum product sales, and minimum product sales.
4. Repeat steps 1 through 3 for *customers.*

Typical sales distribution for quartiles one through four is 89 percent, 7 percent, 3 percent, and 1 percent. Distributions weighted more heavily in quartile 1 suggest greater than average complexity.

Exercise caution when using a quartile in isolation. I have been part of an 80/20 implementation where we cut the bottom two quartiles of products. What happened? We received several "love letters" from our top customers. Turned out, some of those products were "necessary evils," products that must be offered because some of your best customers want them. Quartiles are one-dimensional and tactical but informative. The quads are strategic and powerful.

Create Quads

The segmentation required to identify your most productive 20 percent calls for virtually no subjective decision-making. It is a numbers game.

To play this game, segment your products and customers into four quadrants. Instead of dividing products and customers into four quartiles, use the same force-ranked lists to designate each product/customer as "A" or "B." A products/customers (also known as "80s" products/customers) are those that cumulatively make up 80 percent of sales. The rest are Bs (or "20s").

When you combine the data, you can produce a two-by-two matrix or quad. The top two quadrants of this quad consist of your A customers and the A and B products they buy. The bottom two quads consist of the B customers and the A and B products they buy. (Note, B customers buy mostly B products.) The game's object is to find or devise ways to treat the bottom two quadrants of products and customers differently or eliminate them so that you can free up the company's financial and human assets to concentrate on the top two.

Here's an example:

Products

A = 3,416 Products   B = 31,419 Products

	1	**2**
A = 248 Customers	Total sales = $429,169,262 Sales % = 67.2% Gross Margin = $211,849,951 GM % of Sales = 49.4% Customers = 248 Products = 2,692	Total sales = $82,195,533 Sales % = 12.9% Gross Margin = $5,705,875 GM % of Sales = 6.9% Customers = 233 Products =19,866
	3	**4**
B = 2,062 Customers	Total sales = $83,319,117 Sales % = 13.1% Gross Margin = $39,073,677 GM % of Sales = 46.9% Customers = 1,300 Products = 1,193	Total sales = $43,558,715 Sales % = 6.8% Gross Margin = $19,931,076 GM % of Sales = 45.8% Customers = 1,776 Products = 14,100

Customers

Total revenue for 2009 - 2014 was $638,242,627 with a Gross Margin of $276,560,579.

Fig. 04-01: 80/20 Quad example.

Quadrant 1 in this example reveals that 248 A customers purchased 2,692 products (out of 3,416 A products). The company should, therefore, focus most of its assets and resources on serving these customers and selling these products, which account for 72 percent of sales, for a gross margin of 49.4 percent.

Quadrant 2 reveals that 233 A customers purchased 19,866 out of 31,419 B products. Although A customers are buying more than half of the company's B products, the percentage of total sales is only 12.9 percent, and the gross margin (GM) is just 6.9 percent. The company should devote resources accordingly.

Quadrant 3 at the bottom left shows that 1,300 B customers purchased 1,193 (of 3,416) A products, representing 13.1 percent of sales, which generates a healthy 46.9 GM percentage.

Quadrant 4 shows that 1,776 B customers were the only purchasers of 14,100 B products. These represent a mere 6.8 percent of sales, though the GM percentage of sales is 45.8 percent.

Growth Through Simplification

Analysis of your customer data and product data is aimed at segmenting customers and products into four quadrants so that you can identify your best customers and best products in terms of revenue and GM. This enables the second step in segmentation, *simplification*—reducing complexity in areas important to the business's success.

Essentially, you want to focus more resources on the most productive quadrant (quadrant 1) by identifying your top customers and moving heaven and earth to serve them, selling them the A products they want most. Your greatest opportunity for growth is in selling more A products to more A customers. Secondarily, you will want to focus on quadrant 2, the B products that A customers buy. There are often opportunities to simplify quadrant 2 with mutual benefit to your business and the customer.

As for the bottom two quadrants, which contain B customers,

the strategy is to devote fewer resources to these less productive customers and less profitable products. This is the goal of simplification. It typically involves reducing the number of SKUs on offer, eliminating unproductive ones, and perhaps reducing the number of models in a given product line (especially in quadrant 4). Very importantly, simplification involves diverting your human resources (especially sales personnel) from lengthy interactions with marginally productive B customers.

Will reducing or eliminating personal selling to low-performing B customers mean that you will lose these customers? Yes, at least some of them. And while this sounds like a bad thing—counterintuitive or even malpractice—these are customers you *want* to lose. Servicing them reduces the company's capacity to serve your best customers, sell your best products, cultivate more "A" customers, and create even more "A" products.

The imperative is to prevent your organization from devoting precious resources to improving parts of the business that make little or no positive impact on the business. In business, less is often more. A key lever of performance improvement is reducing—simplifying—the sheer number of products the business offers. While it is very important to identify the 20 percent of products that produce the most revenue, it is even more important to identify the larger number (80 percent) of products that produce a mere 20 percent of revenue. These bottom-quadrant products create unproductive complexity and force the business to spread its resources thin, directing vital assets away from the A products. Profitability is reduced. You lose money by spending more than you take in.

Similarly, as you identify the vital 20 percent of customers who are your best customers, you must identify the bottom 20 percent. To put it bluntly but urgently, you do not want these customers—unless you can retain them with minimal effort and at a worthwhile profit margin. You can require your bottom-quadrant customers to place orders only through the website without intervention from human sales personnel. You can require payment in full upfront by credit or debit card. You can place minimum-order requirements to ensure that your handling costs are covered. You can charge for shipping.

Fire Products and Fire Customers

The Pacific Theater in World War II presented General Douglas MacArthur with a daunting array of military objectives. The Japanese armed forces held an overwhelming number of Pacific islands, and MacArthur had limited ships, men, and weapons to deal with them. So, he made a bold decision. Fight selectively. Instead of trying to capture every Japanese-held island in sequence on the way to the Japanese home islands, strike only at some of the links in the chain and bypass the others, no matter how heavily fortified. By breaking the vital links, those islands left alone would be cut off from their supply chains. They would, as MacArthur put it, "wither on the vine." Starved, they would surrender or die—without the necessity of being beaten into submission by force. By focusing on the key links in the island chains, the progress of counterattacks could be sped up and the loss of men and matériel reduced.

MacArthur applied the principle of simplification, which included disregarding certain island objectives. The same strategy applies to simplifying your business. If you cannot eliminate loss or create meaningful profit with any product, customer, or category of products and customers, fire the product, the customer, or both. I understand that such actions go against the grain of common sense. We naturally assume that if *some* is good, *many* is better. And we believe the old saying, "The customer is always right," as if it had been delivered from the heavens on a blinding bolt of lightning. Moreover, this outright discrimination just doesn't seem fair.

Treating people fairly is important in business, government, and life. But first, you must define "fair." For instance, is it fair to you, your company, your employees, and your customers to compromise quality, service, pricing, and profitability by treating all customers equally? It is fair to do this only if you mistakenly believe that "fair" and "equal" are synonymous.

But they are not—and the strategic objective of 80/20 is not to treat everything and everyone equally but fairly. The fairest thing you can do in business is grow and become better. It benefits every stakeholder, including customers. A business does not grow and improve by devoting 80 percent of its resources to the bottom 20 percent of its products and customers.

Albert Einstein said, "Common sense is nothing more than a deposit of prejudices laid down in the mind before you reach eighteen." As pilots flying in low visibility know that they must trust their instruments over their senses, we in business need to ensure that we think more maturely and sophisticatedly than we did at age eighteen. We need to look at the numbers and trust the numbers. The 80/20 principle will show you not just what products and customers you can live *without* but those you cannot live *with*. These products and customers bleed the lifeblood out of the business. Unprofitable in and of themselves, they also draw your capital and human assets away from the top-quadrant products and customers responsible for 80 percent of whatever success you enjoy.

PART II

Profitable Growth Operating System:
The First Hundred Days in Four Steps

CHAPTER 5

The First Hundred Days: Overview

● ● ●

"A good plan, violently executed now, is better than a perfect plan next week."

—GENERAL GEORGE S. PATTON, JR.

WHEN FRANKLIN DELANO Roosevelt took office on March 4, 1933, during the darkest and most desperate depths of the Great Depression, he revived a phrase born on February 26, 1815, when Napoleon returned to France from exile on Elba. For the next hundred days, he led a stunning military campaign to regain his conquest and throne. Napoleon singlehandedly rebuilt an army of 250,000 and nearly succeeded in retaking his lost empire. Of course, it all ended badly for him a hundred days later at the Battle of Waterloo on June 18, 1815, yet "the hundred days" became a phrase that has continued to echo through history. FDR picked it up 118 years later and put it on himself.

Immediately after his swearing in, President Roosevelt summoned Congress to convene in a three-month-plus special session, during which he presented and gained passage of fifteen precedent-shattering, precedent-making bills, enacting programs aimed at gaining relief from the Great Depression. Goaded and guided by the president, Congress passed a grand total of seventy-seven laws in one hundred days. For those keeping score, that's 0.77 laws per day. It was all too necessary because the United States of America, like much of the world, had become what students of business catastrophe like to call a "burning platform."

Not everybody thinks everything FDR and Congress did in the hundred days was good, but even the critics and outright haters admit that *something* had to be done, and, to this day, the performance of each new occupant of the White House has been judged in some measure on what they achieved or failed to achieve in their first hundred days. I've never had presidential ambitions—if nominated, I will not run. If elected, I will not serve—but, as Roosevelt borrowed from Napoleon, I shamelessly took from Roosevelt when I was called on to serve as CEO of a platform that, while not yet aflame, had begun to smolder. I continually spoke of "the first hundred days."

I applied the first hundred days formula to Phoenix with great and growing success. This other company, let's call it Rolling Thunder Engineered Parts, needed even more urgent intervention. With the best of intentions, it had expanded, but it had done so without a coherent strategy and was thus in urgent need of 80/20 discipline. I worked with the talented executives and dedicated managers of the organization to develop a plan in which we outlined what we intended to do with the first hundred days of *my* administration. I called those first hundred days our "Stub Year." They were all about getting ready. They began what I call "earn the right to grow."

The Four Steps

I wasn't looking to pass seventy-seven laws in one hundred days. We just needed to take *four steps* forward in one hundred days, a span of time in which we could begin to turn our business around:

Step 1: Set the Goal.

This first step (chapter 6) is the easiest and hardest to accomplish.

Size the prize. In private equity, many aim to get at least a 3x multiple on invested cash. Do the math to find what earnings before interest, taxes, depreciation, and amortization (EBITDA) you need to deliver that goal. My company's ambitious goal was to reach $2.3 billion in revenue with 19 percent margins and $300 million in EBITDA within five years.

So, in the first minutes of the first hundred days, we articulated the goal of a five-year plan. This, in turn, implied a more immediate goal: taking the steps necessary to turn the business around and positioning it to earn the right to grow. As I said later during a company town hall, "We will begin by simplifying our business. The executive team has reviewed what to stop, start, and continue doing immediately to get foundationally solid; we will communicate that shortly." I explained that we would collect and use "data to determine where to simplify and grow the business by determining where to raise prices to increase our bottom line."

You and your team must quickly agree on your company's goal. Consider yourself blessed if a sponsor owns your company. Your goal will be found right in your contract. In our case, we needed a strategy that could deliver $300M within our timeframe. If you don't want a planned failure, ensure the math works.

Step 2: Create the Strategy.

The next step (chapter 7) is to identify and build a strategy to achieve the new long-term (for us, it was a five-year goal; some companies think in terms of three). Schedule the strategy meeting within thirty days of the step 1 goal meeting. Since all had to happen so quickly, we relied on the 80/20 principle to identify the roughly 20 percent of what we were doing in our business that was producing 80 percent of our revenue. You should, too. The 80/20 rule lets you speedily separate what is working from what is not. You will want to gather your company's product and customer data immediately.

Do not expect the data to tell you your strategy. You and your team must pick your strategy based on your goal. Unless you are dealing with a total dumpster fire, I strongly suggest you pick a strategy based on winning in your core. The data will not tell you your strategy, but it will tell you the best way to achieve your strategy. Going forward, your decisions must be based on this data-backed knowledge.

Recognize that at the beginning, you may find yourself in a "data puddle," an inch deep and a yard wide. It's still necessary to give clear direction to the team. Your most immediate message to the company should be something like this: *we will have our new roadmap—our new growth-directed strategy—within the first hundred days.* You are seeking progress, not perfection here. As the situation becomes clearer, you should expect to refine your strategy to take advantage of new knowledge.

This is also the time to hold your second company town hall. Give the organization an update on where the team is on the journey. If possible, make this a live event where you can take questions. The boost the team will get with interaction and clarity will amaze you and your team.

Step 3: Build the Structure.

It's been about seventy days, and a lot has happened. The team now has a clear goal and a new, albeit immature, strategy with clearly designated owners. Plus, you have held two company-wide town halls, which have kept everyone in the loop. Oh, and you've been running the business the whole time.

Now comes the most challenging part. If you want to control your business within a hundred days, you probably must reorganize the company (chapter 8). Change is hard under the best of circumstances. It may even be gut-wrenching. People will get new jobs, and some may not have the right skill set. It's often been said, "The definition of insanity is doing the same thing over and over and expecting a different result." Prepare for a change. During the meeting, concentrate on how the business needs to be organized to achieve the strategy. Don't get hung up on which person will do what. This will add unnecessary complexity and bog the process down.

Focus exclusively on structure by strategically segmenting to create great customers, innovate new products, and, most of all, meet your three- to five-year financial goal. The segments of the redesigned business should be organized in a rational structure with provision for accountability for delivering your goals. Prepare to separate unlike businesses and put competent leadership in place to run them. Apply 80/20 to create segments that will direct your most productive resources to your most profitable customers who buy your most profitable products. This will create the strategic growth needed to achieve the goal set in step 1.

Step 4: Launch the Action Plan.

You made it. A hundred days have passed, and it's time to launch the company-wide goal, strategy, and plan to achieve it. Having promised delivery of a new strategy capable of achieving the five-year goal in the first hundred days, you sought to instill a bias for action in the organization.

In my company, at our final town hall of the first hundred days, I said, "We'll define the tactics and efforts to execute the plan. We won't wait for perfection here. We'll make sound, informed decisions and go." In effect, even before the end of the hundred days, we were putting together a rough draft action plan to allow us to make positive decisions and initiate needed actions as soon as possible. The watchword was *progress, not perfection*.

The rough draft action plan must come together even as it is launched. Functional managers throughout the company must quickly put the *action* into action plans for executing the "critical few" objectives in their areas of responsibility. These plans must focus on the 20 percent of customers and 20 percent of products that produce 80 percent of the company's revenue. In parallel, upper-level executives must press ahead with the overall, long-term company-wide strategy. A working version of the strategy should be in place by the end of the first hundred days, but the full strategic management process (SMP) will require a year, a journey through all four reporting quarters, to bring to its first maturity. This is the process you should intend to ride the rest of the way to your three- to five-year goal.

From Fireside Chat to Town Hall

The first hundred days is not self-executing, and it does not run on automatic pilot. Communication is at its heart. Franklin Roosevelt had his celebrated fireside chats, in which he talked to the American people in a frank and friendly manner via radio broadcast, sharing with them the government's short-term and long-term plans. Our company had town halls rather than fireside chats, in which executives and managers at all levels came together. The first town hall kicked off the first hundred days. At the end of month one, we convened another town hall to review and measure our progress, monitor our course, and make any necessary corrections. As in the first town hall, the second half of the meeting was devoted to questions and answers. The third meeting came near the end of the first hundred days and coincided with the end of the first quarter, the regular occasion for reports and evaluation. In this way, the first hundred days merged naturally with the regular running of the business. Yet, unquestionably, everyone understood that, by this point, we had introduced something entirely new into the business: a complete strategy and process for a turnaround intended to earn us the right to grow.

Beyond the First Hundred Days

The first hundred days accommodate a four-step process

intended to set up the next full year in the context of a longer-term plan, often a five-year plan, sometimes a three-year plan. Now, since that plan evolves and changes during the first full year and over the entire three- to five-year span, you should not be focused narrowly on the hundred days before you. Or, rather, think of the timeframe this way:

1. What you accomplish in the first hundred days must accurately aim and successfully launch an effort to *earn the right to grow*. This effort will be the focus of year one of a five-year plan. The principal action in this first year is applying 80/20 to simplify the business, returning to profitable basics, the 20 percent of inputs (products, customers, personnel, actions, initiatives) that produce 80 percent of your revenue.

2. If your launch is successful and your first year earns your company the right to grow, your second year will be dedicated to growing profitably by taking market share from the competition. This requires relentlessly applying 80/20 to ensure the company's *focus on the critical few*: products, customers, markets, personnel, and initiatives—in short, simplifying all the company's investment of resources to those inputs that will produce profitable growth.

3. Having begun to exercise the right to grow in year two, the theme of year three is *double down*. You now have sufficient data to tell you what is and is not working. Invest in what is working.

4. Year four is a span in which to *polish* your success by fine-tuning all your processes to reduce waste and grow profits further.

5. Year five is the *flywheel* toward which the entire progressive growth OS is oriented. In many mechanical

vehicles and devices, the flywheel is a weighted wheel that exploits the physical law of conservation of angular momentum to store rotational energy and thus optimize the machine's momentum to accelerate movement and/or provide a reserve of available power that stabilizes the machine's operation and even keeps it moving despite temporary interruptions in external power. Translated to business activity, the flywheel is an incremental increase in efficiency that accelerates and sustains growth.

CHAPTER 6

Step 1: Set a Goal

⬡ ⬡ ⬡

"If you do not think about the future, you cannot have one."

—JOHN GALSWORTHY, *Swan Song* (1928)

A SURPRISING NUMBER of people find these three words terrifying: *set a goal*. Some are overwhelmed by the range of possibilities, and others are discouraged by a dearth of options. Me? I never sweat it, and you don't have to, either. You can always set a goal in the language of business—the language of money. When the private equity company I work with hired me to become CEO of an underperforming company it had bought, that's just the language I led our executive leadership team in speaking.

Rolling Thunder Engineered Parts, introduced in the preceding chapter, is a large distributor of aftermarket parts for various vehicles, from motorcycles and ATVs to outdoor power equipment to light vehicles. It covers the United States and thirteen other countries in South America, Europe, and Asia, expanding in kudzu fashion regarding markets, products, and geographical spread.

The one thing missing? Strategy.

Strategic growth—that is, *profitable* growth—is always good. Growth in and of itself, however, can turn out to be good, bad, or indifferent, which is just another word for bad. For too many years, Rolling Thunder had been dodging strategic growth by focusing on acquisitions. The pandemic had delivered extraordinary growth, and now the party was over. People were going back to work. The result was that it was soon rolling toward a declining market. When I entered the company, its most recent history was marked by declining financial results.

The company's people were not stupid. They just hadn't been paying attention, not to the business or each other. Some were pulling, others were pushing, and many were struggling just to stand in place. Now, people start businesses for different reasons. Some have a passion for a particular product or industry. Some have a family tradition to honor. Some have certain moral or philanthropic motives. Private equity, which employed me, just wanted to make money. They buy a company low, grow it, and then sell it high. That's their basic business model. It is by no means a cynical or craven model. To buy low and sell high requires adding value to the company, which calls for astute and earnest stewardship of the enterprise with a level of management that makes the company better. This is a goal and achievement that benefits all stakeholders.

Moreover, adding value to increase the sales price is a very clear and straightforward purpose. That doesn't make it easy to achieve, but it does make it easy to understand. So, when my firm put me into Rolling Thunder as CEO, my assignment was sufficiently straightforward to declare in a single imperative sentence: *turn it around.*

Turn it around. That was my purpose. Okay, but where did we need to go? Speaking the language of money, I set a financial goal for Rolling Thunder: to reach $2.3 billion in revenue, have 18 percent margins, and $300 million in EBITDA within five years. With that goal up in lights, step 1 was done.

I had allocated ten days of the first hundred days to set a

goal for the turnaround. Did we need all ten days to develop something that can be stated in a single sentence containing just three numbers?

In fact, writing it down took about ten seconds, but preparing to write it called for getting a high-level view of the company's performance and then asking questions of leaders at both the executive and operational level. That kind of walking around does take some time. Also, a goal is a *what*—*what* we must achieve. We also had to broadly outline a *how*—*how* we were going to win that goal. So, almost immediately after the leadership core meeting in which the goal was set, I called our first town hall meeting, at which the goal was presented. At both the town hall and in a summary open letter to the organization following it, I explained, "We will begin by *simplifying our business*. The executive team has reviewed what to stop, start, and continue doing immediately to get foundationally solid; we will communicate that shortly." Then I added the process that is key to any *simplification,* namely, an 80/20 process. We will, I explained, use "data to determine where to simplify and grow the business by determining where to raise prices to increase our bottom line."

Goooooooal! Out of What Did I Pull My Numbers?

The goal. Where did it come from? Thin air? My... hat? First, understand that the most important thing about the goal is that *it is a goal*, something we didn't have before. The numbers—$2.3 billion in revenue, 18 percent margins, $300 million in EBITDA within five years—are just numbers. Maybe they are precisely the right numbers. Maybe we could have come up with better numbers. At least they aren't the wrong numbers because they are not facts but aspirations that have yet to be fulfilled as facts. They are good aspirations, ambitious but possible, even feasible, and perhaps even reasonable. The goal we chose makes a good target, and though an unaimed arrow never misses, it never hits anything you want to hit on purpose. So, the specific numbers aside, the goal provides a target, which provides a direction, which brings order where there was none and replaces panic with hope.

When you are called on to turn a company around, you are inevitably torn in two opposite directions. On the one hand, you are supposed to have all the answers. On the other, if you are convinced that you have all the answers, you won't learn anything about the company you are expected not only to save but to grow profitably. If you think you already know it all, you won't be inclined to look and listen, make yourself understand the company's culture, and learn about its history, processes, and expectations. You won't be inclined to learn about its people.

In this project to unlock value, glancing at quarterly reports made it easy to see that the company was suffering from declining financial results. I also saw a whole lot of projects and initiatives underway. The kneejerk response is to give three cheers. After all, doing stuff is better than not doing stuff. Right? And doing a lot of stuff has to be even better.

Well, not when most of the stuff is unaccompanied by strategic consideration of return on investment. Doing stuff costs money. The more stuff you do, the more money it costs. And it appeared that nobody was paying much attention to cash flow. Financial data, analytics, KPI, and tracking capabilities ranged from inadequate to nil. Tax issues, including add-back limitations, severance obligations, and contractual cash requirements, were all ignored even though they contributed to an increasingly dismal cash situation.

The key to a pilot flying an airplane is acquiring and maintaining situational awareness. For executives piloting a business, the most foundational requirement for acquiring and maintaining situational awareness is having a firm handle on cash flow. As the pilot, you need to know where you are going, how fast, how far, how much fuel, and, oh, yeah, whether you are flying right side up or inverted. Nothing of this level of awareness was evident at Rolling Thunder. It wasn't a case of bad luck. It was a bad strategy—or none. As things were going, there were not very many levers left to yank. The thing is—when you walk into a situation in which a lot is going on in all directions (all of them pretty much wrong), and the only thing that is crystal clear is that the organization is running out of gas—it's easy to get overwhelmed by panic and despair. That is an understandable response, but it is a combination that creates confusion, breeds pessimism, dissolves morale, and creates paralysis.

Having reviewed and read all that I could, I held that first core meeting with the upper management team, asked them questions, and then worked with them to set a goal that would (if it could be reached) turn the company around, creating the value that would reverse the decline. To unwind the segments of the company that were hurting us and then refocus our resources on what was performing well or showed sufficient promise to rehabilitate would take time and study. What we needed right now were plausible numbers that could turn us around. So, together, we set our five-year goal. Based on historical and current performance, we had no reason to believe we could reach that goal. But the goal did give us the numbers we had to make to achieve our goal in five years. Possessing this goal demanded that we figure out our "go-get," precisely what we needed to reach the goal.

Town Hall Time

Almost immediately after that first core meeting with the executive leadership team, I convened the first company-wide town hall. In this case, it was a combined in-person and virtual meeting because it involved some 3,600 participants distributed over about forty locations. The meeting was scheduled to last two hours. In the first sixty minutes, I delivered a status report and stated the goal the executive leadership team and I had set. I told the truth—that we were missing sales targets and our costs were increasing. I stated flatly that we had to take immediate action to start hitting our targets while reducing costs. We needed to "steady the company," I said. I explained that we would act quickly to cut spending and initiatives not tied to revenue generation. This would enable us to focus on the most important priorities for our success.

After delivering the unvarnished truth, the bad, the ugly, and the good—because there is always good—I told the employees exactly what I intended to do, which was to perform the four steps I am outlining in this section of this book. These four steps, I explained, will enable us to turn the company around together so that we can earn the right to grow.

The entire second hour of the town hall was devoted to answering questions from the participants. With sales, cash, and morale on a downward trajectory, time is my enemy. The first hundred days are about accelerating change and rapidly earning the right to grow. Another way to accelerate my learning about the company was to draw up and circulate a questionnaire in advance of the town hall in which I asked employees to answer as many questions as possible. I ensured that we discussed their answers before the town hall so that I could read them. I chose certain questions to bring up and discuss in the town hall. After this, time permitting, I opened the proceedings to spontaneous questions.

Accelerate Your Learning with a Questionnaire
QUESTIONS TO ASK ABOUT THE PAST
Performance

1. How well or poorly has the company performed in the past?
2. What goals were set?
3. What kind of benchmarks were employed?

4. What actions were taken when goals were not reached?
5. What initiatives for change were made in the past?
6. Who was most responsible for change initiatives?
7. How effective or ineffective were these attempts at change?
8. What drivers have had a positive impact on performance? Why?
9. What drivers have had a negative impact on performance? Why?
10. How have the company's strategy, structure, technical capabilities, culture, and politics impacted performance?

QUESTIONS TO ASK ABOUT THE PRESENT
Vision and Strategy

1. Does the company have a clear vision statement? If so, what is it?
2. Does the company have a clear articulation of strategy? If so, what is it?
3. Is the company's strategy being executed optimally?
4. If not, why not? If so, will this strategy win?

The Team

1. Who is exceptional?
2. Who is competent and capable?
3. Who is not competent and capable?
4. Who deserves the company's total confidence?
5. Who does not deserve the company's total confidence?
6. Who are the influencers on the team? What are the sources of their influence?

Company Policies and Processes

1. What are the company's most significant practices and processes?

2. Do the essential practices and processes promote value, productivity, and safety?

3. What can be done to improve performance of practices and processes?

Latent Risks and Hazards

1. Are there latent risks and hazards that threaten the performance of the company?

2. Is the company subject to cultural/political risks or peril? What are they?

Easy Victories to Score

1. Where and what are business areas in which easy and early wins can be scored?

QUESTIONS ABOUT THE FUTURE
Near-Future Challenges and Problems

1. What challenges and problems will the business likely encounter in the coming year?

2. How should we prepare to meet and overcome them?

Near-Future Opportunities

1. What unexploited opportunities lie ahead? What do we need to realize them?

Obstacles

1. What significant obstacles do we face ahead?

2. What do we need to do now to prepare to overcome these obstacles?

Company Culture

1. Is the company culture in need of change?

2. Which aspects of the company culture should be

preserved? Which aspects should be changed?

Following the first core meeting and town hall, having seen, heard, and learned a lot about the company, I met with the entire team and recapped much I had said at the town hall. "I'd like to share a bit about where we are now," I began, "where we're going, and how we'll get there." I never wagged my finger, and I certainly did not get personal. I repeated the truths I had told at the town hall about how the company was missing sales targets despite increasing costs. I aimed to accelerate the forging of a bond with the organization by telling the truth about the difficulties we faced and the countervailing truth that we were capable of achieving our goal together.

Even in a hard situation, the truth, painful as it may be, has great positive power. This lesson was learned and shared by Admiral Jim Stockdale, which I presented in chapter 2. Those who survived, with him, horrific incarceration as POWs in the Vietnam War did so by facing facts, avoiding complacency and wishful thinking, and never losing confidence that they would ultimately prevail. As Stockdale explained to Jim Collins, you cannot let wishfully optimistic thinking cause you to abandon the "discipline to confront the most brutal facts of your current reality, whatever they might be." This "Stockdale Paradox" helps you maintain the discipline to find your way through the worst problems. What you need is a *process* and the discipline to follow that process. Process can mean the difference between rational hope and panic-stricken despair.

Panic and despair are the products of inaction, a sense of not knowing what to do, a feeling of being unable to do anything, certainly anything capable of *turning it around*. So, when I walk into an underperforming company, I aim to give the people something to do. I provide direction. As is often the case when I am called in, the first thing or first few things that need doing are starkly obvious. The house is burning, so you put out the fire.

The boat is leaking, so you plug the holes. I repeated in my letter what I had said at the town hall: "We will quickly cut spending and initiatives not tied to revenue generation to provide a laser focus on the most important priorities for our success."

After this, I invited the whole team to look, with me, to the future. That was especially important because these folks were far from certain they had any future, at least not with Rolling Thunder. I did not promise anyone that they would succeed, but I did promise them effective change: "Over the next few days, weeks, and months, we'll implement many changes to secure this company's health."

Even by itself, promising change is important because the one thing most people in a distressed or declining organization clearly understand is that they need change. If they give it even a little thought, they also understand—without anyone having to tell them—that to make tomorrow different from today, they must do something different today. In the letter, I spelled out the four steps that would enable the changes. As I put it, "These changes will be tied to my four-step system, which takes three to four months to complete." I chose the word *system* deliberately because it is far more compelling than *plan*. A *system* is a set of principles and procedures that tell everyone how to do something. A *system* is a well-organized framework, a tested method. A *plan*, in contrast, expresses an aspiration, a hope, an intention. Modify the word *system* with *four-step,* and you endow that system with a lot of exactitude. It is *four* steps, not *three*, not *five*, and certainly not *several* or a *bunch*. The specificity endowed my solution with instant credibility. Framing the system in terms of time was even more impactful: three to four months.

Why did I go out of my way to call it *my* four-step system? Full disclosure, the "system" is hardly unique to me, but I claimed ownership of it because I have repeatedly used it successfully. The possessive pronoun is my promise to an organization that

I understand the system, have expertise in implementing the system, and accept personal accountability for the system. To each organization I lead in this first step, I promise my accountability. It is the one thing I know beyond doubt that I control.

CHAPTER 7

Step 2: Create the Strategy

◆ ◆ ◆

"It is a bad plan that admits no modification."

—*PUBLIUS SYRUS*, MAXIMS, first century BC

STEP 1 SETS a goal. That identifies *what* is to be done and points to the necessary strategy: *how* to do it. When turnaround is imperative, simplification is the strategy. Company-wide, this means using the 80/20 principle to identify what is working and what is not working so that management can move resources from *what is not* working to *what is*.

Step 2 is to *create the strategy* that will position the company to earn the right to grow. A hundred-day turnaround timeline goes by fast, so speed is of the essence. The sooner the course correction is implemented, the sooner the cash flow bleeding will stop. Don't expect the draft of the strategy produced in the span of step 2 to guide the company for all time. You just need it to propel the business to step 3, in which the executive and operational leadership puts some meat on the strategic bones and gives the business a new structure going forward, one that will enable, facilitate, and accelerate optimum focus on customer base and product offering to drive profitable growth.

Step 2 does not promise perfection, just progress. The strategy that emerges from step 2 is intended to be modified going forward in response to the changing demands of reality. Like steps 1 and 3, step 2 is a step toward lifting the organization to step 4: an action plan.

Schedule the step 2 strategy meeting within thirty days of the step 1 goal meeting. Use the 80/20 principle to identify the roughly 20 percent of what you are doing in your business that is producing 80 percent of your revenue. Knowing this enables you to speedily separate what is working from what is not. You will want to gather your company's product and customer data immediately.

Data alone will not tell you your strategy. You and your team must pick your strategy based on the goal set in step 1. Unless you are in the midst of a rapidly moving disaster, pick a strategy focused on winning at your core. Make the foundation of your strategy a play to your core strengths. Once you have decided on this as your strategy, the data will tell you the best way to achieve it. From this point forward, your decisions must be based on this data-backed knowledge.

The way to delineate your core is to apply 80/20 simplification to identify what is working and what is not and separate the two so that management can move resources from one to the other. This will rather rapidly position the company to earn the right to grow. Bear in mind that you are, in the first hundred days, prioritizing speed. The tradeoff is perfection. So, the strategic draft you are creating in a handful of days is not meant to guide the company through the ages but merely to propel it to the next step, step 3, in which the executive and operational leadership gives body to the strategy in the form of a structure for the company going forward, a structure to enable, facilitate, and accelerate optimum focus on the customers and products that will create profitable growth before the end of the first full year.

The strategy that should emerge from step 2 is a plan deliberately intended to be modified going forward as reality demands. Step 2, like step 1 and step 3, is intended to lift the organization to step 4, an action plan. That will be the juiciest fruit of the first hundred days.

Setting a goal in step 1 required assessing the historical and current situation of the company with an eye toward the future. The formula that informs step 1 informs all four steps outlined in part II: *to make tomorrow different from today, do something different today.* Now, to generate the major objectives and initiatives to achieve the goal set in step 1, you must translate the insights gained from the situation assessment into a strategic framework to build a structure capable of strategically executing toward your goal.

Step 2 in the PGOS generally unfolds in a series of meetings among members of the management team. They analyze the most recent data, comparing it to data gathered over the prior year, and they use the resulting framework to drive the decisions that will guide the strategic structure to be created in step 3. In the framework of step 2, the leadership team decides what exactly is needed—the objectives that must be achieved—to reach the company's long-term (three- to five-year) goal. Once the objectives are articulated, alignment of the organization on those objectives must be secured.

Think of the strategy as the scaffold on which the business plan is drawn up and delivered to the organization. As it is hammered together in step 2, the strategic framework lays out the objectives and initiatives required to realize them. The articulation of the strategy must answer five big questions:

1. What is needed to achieve breakthrough growth and/or performance?
2. What are the differentiators required to win?
3. What are the strategic opportunities or issues? Consider, for example, new product development, line extension, acquisitions, etc.

4. What are the highest-value opportunities? Consider, for example, the potential of new product lines and their affordability.

5. With questions 1 through 5 answered, ask and answer: *what are the critical few initiatives to prioritize?*

Working the Framework

The 80/20 framework positions managers to create a business plan built upon the organization's strategic alignment on "critical few" priorities. With strategic alignment established, the next step is to frame a cross-functional execution to achieve profitable organic growth. Once this coordinated execution plan is in place, the framework positions the team to invest in growth through geographic and line expansion. Coordinated workflows are best plotted and presented graphically. By way of example, here is a chart I used at Phoenix to lay out the workflow of an 80/20 PGOS strategic framework:

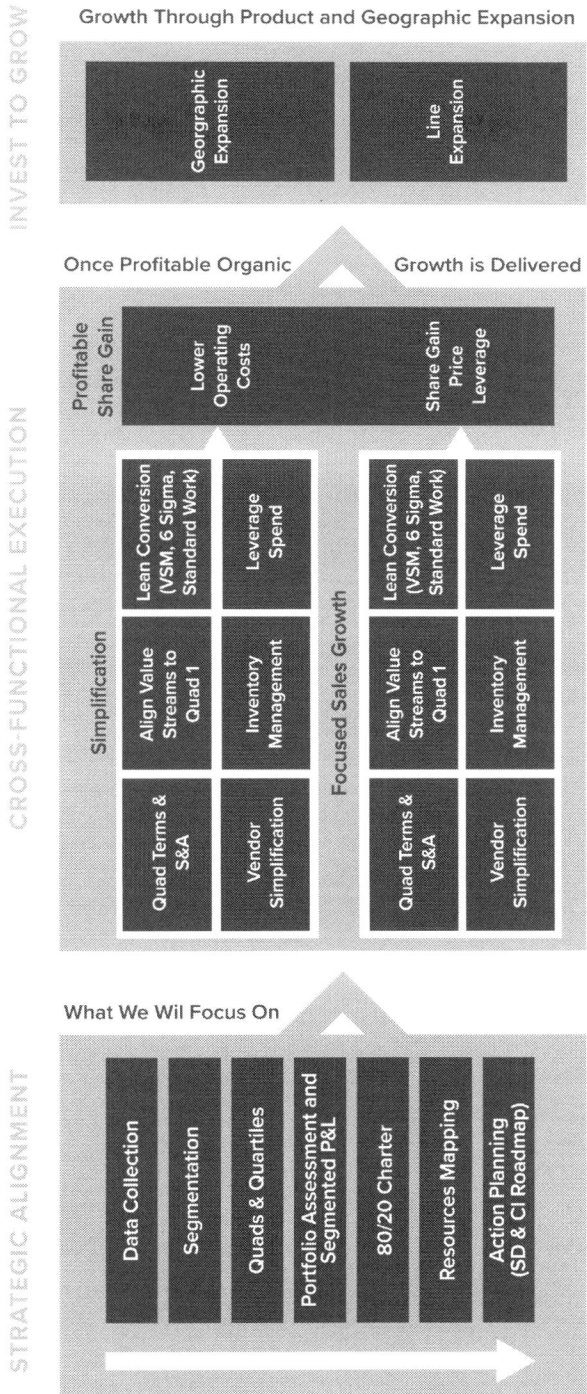

Fig. 07-01: Strategic alignment.

Strategic alignment begins with data collection. In our digitized age, data has never been more abundant. Data is gathered and segmented into quadrants, as explained in chapter 4. Once the top 20 percent and remaining quadrants are identified, they are included in a quad, which consists of these four quadrants:

1. The quadrant of A customers matched up with the A products they buy is placed in the upper left corner of the quad, which is often called The Fort.
2. A customer/B product combinations are put into quadrant 2, which is often called the necessary evil.
3. B customer/A product combinations are segmented into quadrant 3, which is reserved for "transactional business."
4. B customer/B product combinations are relegated to quadrant 4, a segment that must either be priced up or exited from.

Segmentation aims to show you how to appropriately treat each customer/product quad to allocate resources strategically. Here, "strategically" means treating the customers and products in each quadrant in ways that optimize profit margin. This begins by ensuring that the Fort is optimally served by making it the prime focus of resources. Once quadrant 1 is adequately allocated, the leadership team can strategically allocate the remaining available resources to quadrants 2 and 3.

In quadrant 2, the objective is to *sufficiently* serve the A customers who buy B products. "Sufficiently" means devoting to these customers neither more nor less than a level of service that ensures you retain them and that the B products perform as well as *B products* can. This is why we call this quadrant the necessary evil.

You must do all you can to retain your A customers and position the company to either convert customers up from the current B ranks or acquire even more (that is, new) A customers from the outside.

For the B customers buying A products in quadrant 3, the objective is to facilitate sales using minimal resources. Business in this segment is opportunistic rather than strategic. It should, therefore, be transactionally focused rather than relationship focused. Use digital technology to handle these sales online through machines and software rather than human employee interaction.

Finally, customers and products in the bottom right quadrant, quadrant 4, must be treated with a combination of price increases, resource reduction, and sales restrictions (such as requiring minimum purchases, online sales only, credit/debit card purchases only, etc.) to cut to the bone the cost of selling. Products that cannot be sufficiently priced up in these ways or by simply raising the purchase price must be eliminated. You cannot afford to invest resources and other overhead in products that don't make a profit. If they don't *make* money, they *lose* money, meaning they are killing you. You will lose customers when you drop these products, but those customers are killing you, so your company benefits from their departure.

Handling quad 4 gives some managers qualms of conscience. They may feel that treating one set of customers differently from another is *unfair*. This is not true. While the treatment is *unequal*, it is not *unfair*. The treatment is appropriately *unequal* because an A customer is quantitatively different from a B customer. That is, the two are not equals—not as customers, anyway—and since your treatment of them is not as people but as customers, treating them *unequally* is not the same as treating them *unfairly*. To treat a productive customer as a nonproductive customer would certainly be unfair, however, to your best customers and your company.

Having segmented customers and products and then

assembled the individual quadrants into quads, the team must dive deeper to analyze the company's portfolio as a segmented profit and loss (P&L) statement. For example, say your analysis reaches these conclusions about the four quadrants:

> Quadrant 1: 64 percent of total revenue; 200 percent of total profit
> Quadrant 2: 16 percent of total revenue; break-even profit
> Quadrant 3: 16 percent of total revenue; 20 percent of total profit
> Quadrant 4: 4 percent of total revenue; a -120 percent loss (It is killing you.)

For 80/20, profit is calculated as profit [+] and loss [-]. In business, as in arithmetic, negative numbers are just as real as positive numbers. So, quadrant 1 and quadrant 3 produce 220 percent of the company's profit. But quadrant 2 is a wash, breaking even with zero profit and zero loss, and quadrant 4 is responsible for a negative profit (a loss) of -120 percent. The company portrayed here is a four-cylinder automobile putting along on just one cylinder (quadrant 1), with two (quadrants 2 and 3) barely pulling their weight, and one (quadrant 4) representing a real drag.

The deeper-dive analysis needs to sort actual product categories (or even SKUs) into each quadrant so that the performance of the company's portfolio may be critically assessed at a granular level. This leads to a more meaningful discussion aimed at formulating an "80/20 charter," which answers the question, "What products/product categories are we going to retain to create an optimal portfolio?" In other words, *On what, exactly, will we focus?*

Your executive leadership team and managers probably will not be able to make a complete analysis in the first one hundred days. No matter what, get enough data and sufficient analysis to chart general trends. This will be sufficient to make good decisions on which to base good actions. Once you implement the strategy through action, you will produce measurable results that will guide you over the next full year in modifying your business and action plans. As the Latin writer Publius Syrus observed in the first century BC, "It is a bad plan that admits no modification."

Cross-Functional Execution

From strategic alignment, the team moves to cross-functional execution. This requires the application of two priorities: simplification and focused sales growth. Both operate on the 80/20 principle. Essentially, the task is to devise ways to optimally allocate approximately 80 percent of your resources to quadrant 1. The obvious place to draw additional human resources to service that top quadrant is quadrant 4, where these resources are disproportionately squandered in futile and costly service to low-performing customers and products. In addition, you will want to do all you can to reduce friction and increase efficiency throughout the organization. For example:

- Formulate the terms and service level agreement (SLA) for each quadrant, such that you always serve quadrant 1 most intensively.
- Align all value streams to quadrant 1.
- Apply lean (see chapter 13) and other efficiency and continuous improvement standards to all operations and processes.
- Simplify your stable of vendors, consolidating them and reducing their number so that you can secure volume pricing.
- Improve inventory management with such practices as just-in-time (JIT) and the like.

- Leverage your spending with strategic discipline.

These actions will lower operating costs and overhead in ways that can be expected to produce a gain in profitable shares.

Creating focused sales growth requires aligning your go-to-market strategy with the quadrants. Quadrant 1 demands—and must receive!—the most resource-intensive strategy, including (for example) consultative selling and such value-adding services as installation and calibration. Properly focusing the growth (that is, the profitability) of sales almost invariably requires simplification of product lines, concentrating on A lines that contribute to the high-performing 80s. Pricing should be strategic, with levels of customers, minimum-order levels, automatic reorders, and the like influencing the determination of what prices are offered to which customers. Quadrant terms and SLAs must always favor quadrant 1, with growth initiatives focused on 80s products and 80s customers.

The actions taken in the name of focused sales growth should all aim to achieve market share gain and leverage prices to create profitable *organic* growth. Once this is secured, the 80/20 framework can be applied to growth outside the organic bounds. This includes investment in geographic expansion and product line expansion.

Prioritize Sure Things and Worthwhile Wins

The 80/20 principle can determine product/customer segments with the clearest path to success. This is not to be confused with going after low-hanging fruit. Rather (to continue the fruit metaphor), it is all about identifying those products in the portfolio and those customers in the whole customer base who possess sufficient juice to make the squeeze worthwhile.

It is good to win anytime, but it is always best to win early. This builds both momentum and confidence. One of the companies I lead consists of four component groups. Let's call them ABC,

DEF, GHI, and JKL. We determined which of these groups had the clearest path to success.

A. ABC, which supplies a commodity as a service, possessed many of the focused qualities that gave it the best path to success when we studied it.

B. DEF was hobbled by an entrenched "administrative state" and many priorities. There was work yet to be done to fix it.

C. GHI had too many priorities and may have been afflicted with an inefficient but entrenched administrative state. Again, there is work to be done here.

D. JKL was well run but selling into a mature market with a visible horizon. This one was a candidate for possible closure or inclusion (at a simplified level) in another unit.

It was apparent that ABC demanded the highest-priority attention—not because it was doing poorly (the contrary was the case) but because it was an 80s performer and thus a source of significant profit that was there for the taking and growing.

Key Ratios

A common way to determine which company or component has the clearest path to success is to analyze key ratios. Typical key ratios to look at include:

- **Working capital ratio:** Dividing current assets by current liabilities reveals how capable a company is of meeting current financial obligations.
- **Price-Earnings (P/E) Ratio:** Dividing current stock price by earnings per share yields the price investors pay for $1 of a company's profit.

- **Return on assets:** Dividing net income by total assets reveals what percentage of profit a company earns versus its available resources.
- **Return on equity:** Dividing net income by shareholders' equity indicates how efficiently management uses investors' capital.

Useful Output

As applied to creating the strategy preparatory to *building the structure (step 3) and launching the action plan (step 4)*, the output of the 80/20 framework after step 2 should end with a clear summary (based on an 80/20 analysis) of where the organization will compete, how it will compete, what capabilities are required to compete, and why the organization will win. The results of the analysis must be evaluated in the context of the goal (the numbers required to turn the company around and earn the right to grow), the current mission and vision of the company, and the historical data that indicates prior performance trends. The output of step 2 must specify the recommended strategic imperatives and priorities. Recognizing that the work of the first hundred days is to provide a course of action subject to modification and correction—that is, make progress, not achieve perfection—each priority and imperative should be defined with specific reference to rationale and scoping and any available discussion of value-at-risk vs. value-creation potential. A good rule of thumb for the output of step 2 is to relate each strategic priority to three to five strategic initiatives aimed at all or any of the following: strengthening the core (corresponding to the Fort), improving market attractiveness, and improving competitive position.

CHAPTER 8

Step 3: Build the Structure

"Things have to be made to happen in the way you want them to happen."

—BLAISE PASCAL, *Pensées* (no, 505), 1670

ALL FOUR STEPS taken in the first hundred days move toward the creation of a business plan and an action plan. Step 3, *build the structure*, is the heart of the business plan, and in step 4, we *launch the action plan* to begin executing the strategy. Of course, the business plan at this point is in an early, partial iteration, subject to change as the plan is tested against the reality of the next three to five years.

The structure that emerges from step 3 is designed to transform the strategy outlined in step 2, *create the strategy*, into an actionable plan. The vehicle of transformation is an 80/20 analysis that organizes the business into segments to create the optimum focus on only those customers and products that will yield strategic growth. In chapter 7, I offered a graphical illustration of an 80/20 framework. Let us repeat it here:

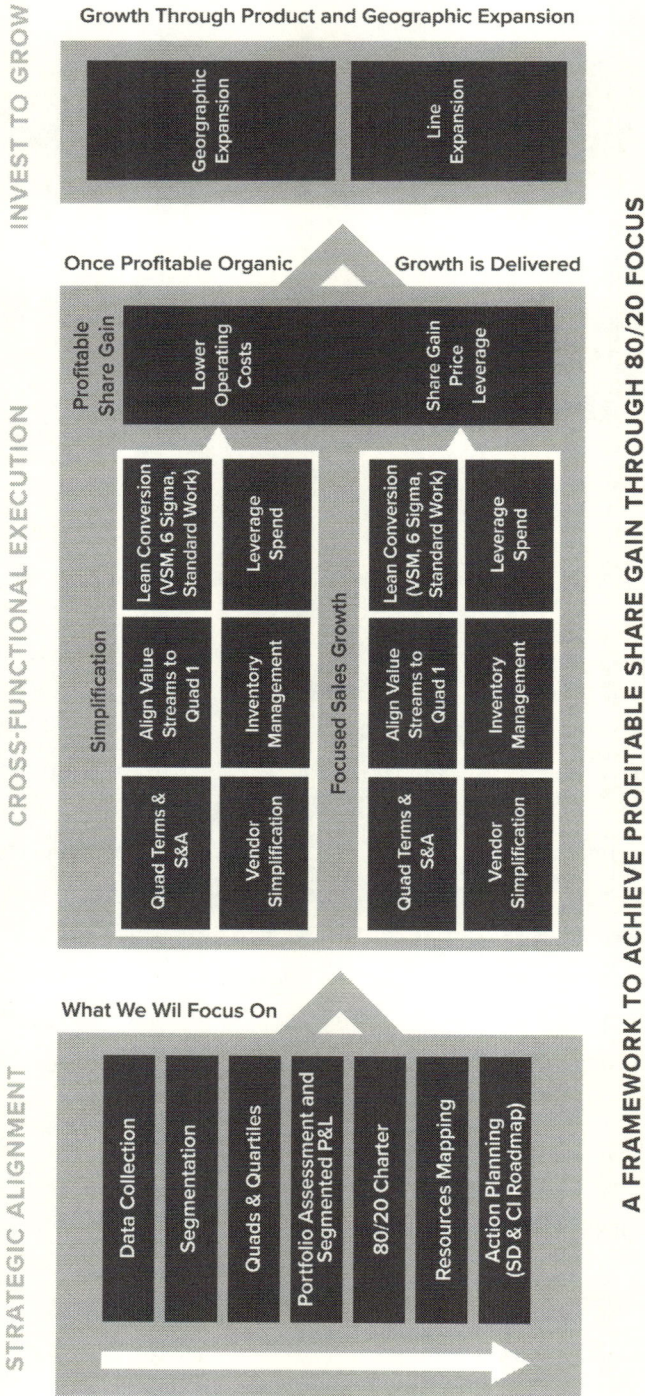

Fig. 08-01: Example of 80/20 Framework workflow.

Step 2 includes strategic alignment—determining the focus of the company toward delivering profitable organic growth—and the cross-functional execution of that focus. Step 3 builds on both strategic alignment and cross-functional execution, supplying *how* these functions will be carried out to achieve profitable share gain in the market by lowering operating costs and growing sales organically. Step 3 also takes the company beyond the point at which profitable organic growth is delivered and outlines a plan for investing in further growth through geographic (territory) and product line expansion. The entire sequence in this business plan is governed by applying the 80/20 principle to ensure strategic allocation of resources.

Use Divergent and Convergent Thinking

The 80/20 principle is remarkably clear and prescriptive. Strictly by the numbers, it will tell you what to do. It will not, however, tell you how to do it. As with many rule-based procedures, thinking is still required. We discussed divergent and convergent thinking in chapter 3. Starting with divergent thinking, brainstorm on the insights you gleaned from your situation assessment in steps 1 and 2. The objective is to evaluate the implications of your assessment and inventory and assess the viable strategic options available to the business for achieving the goal set in step 1. Work to devise options in the following areas:

- Adjacencies
- New market and product development
- Acquisitions and divestiture
- Network/footprint
- Make/buy
- New capabilities
- Core business improvement
- Improving market attractiveness

- Improving competitive position

Having inventoried what is possible, shift from divergent to convergent thinking. Filter your brainstorming laundry list to a short list containing only the imperative issues and highest-value opportunities. Use this list to deliver statements of strategic objectives and strategic initiatives. The deliverables of the convergent thinking process are statements of strategic objectives and strategic initiatives—that is, a preview of the actions needed to execute on the objectives. The goal of convergent thinking is to produce a strategy that fully answers three questions:

1. Where will we compete?
2. How will we compete?
3. How will we win?

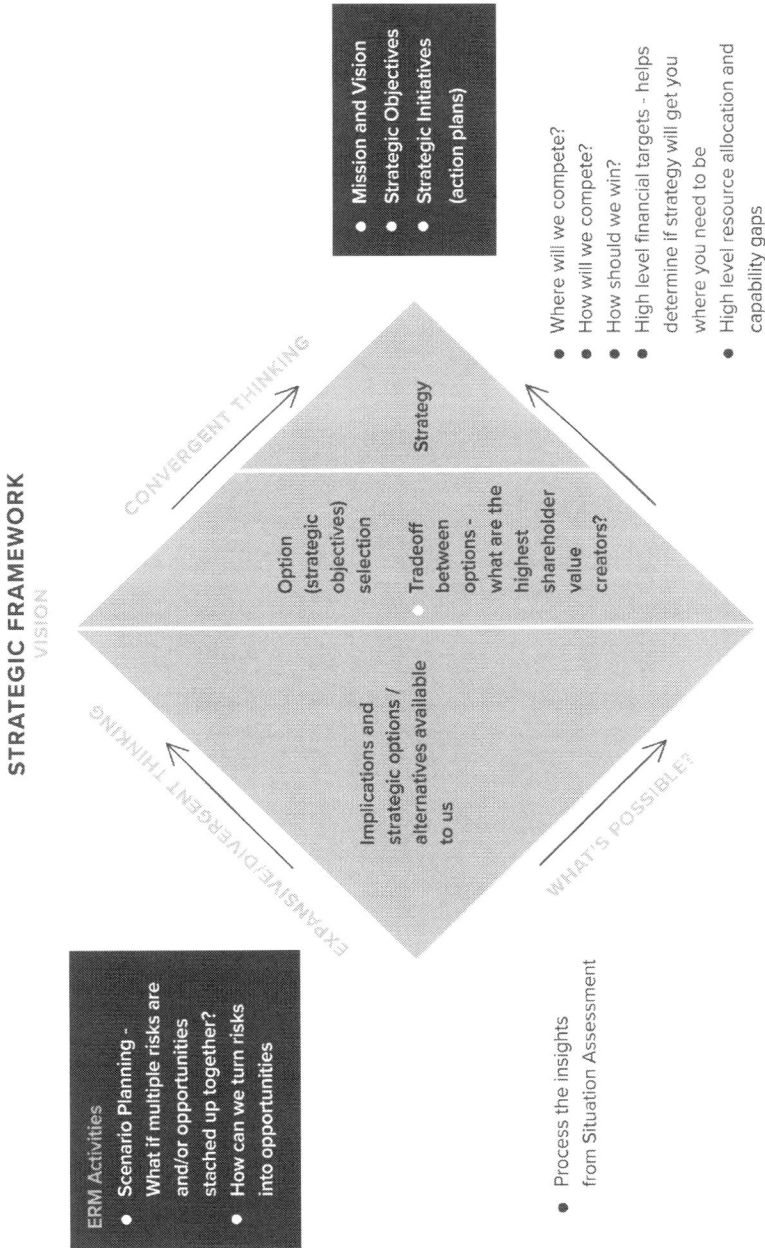

Fig. 08-02: Roles of Divergent and Convergent thinking.

Back in step 1, you set a three- or five-year *company-wide* financial goal. You are now in position to do an initial formulation of specific financial targets in *each sector* of the business and/ or for *each product line.* This formulation will audit the overall strategy, assessing whether it has a fair chance of reaching your step 1 goal. If there is a shortfall, indicating that the present form of the strategy will not reach the goal, look for and identify any resource allocation and capability gaps. To bridge these gaps, determine what additional resources can be moved from quads 2 through 4 to serve quadrant 1 customers and products. Next, enumerate the trade-offs among the available options you have identified. Using your 80/20 results, focus on those likely to produce the greatest profitability. These are the key strategic objectives to retain for the business plan.

Convergent thinking is about zeroing in on the best options. Filter out all but the highest-value opportunities by looking at their revenue and profit potential, affordability, and relative ease of execution in the context of the company's available core competencies and strategic assets (CCSAs). Next, filter the result from the first cut until you are left with the "critical few" (generally three to five) strategic initiatives required to attain your objectives. With respect to each of these initiatives, the convergent thinking sessions should enumerate:

1. The critical changes needed
2. Financial analysis and projections
3. Resource requirements
4. Risk assessments

When you have narrowed your focus to key programs and projects, as well as the actions, resources, organizational implications, and investments required to execute the strategic priorities, evaluate each within a quick-and-dirty long-term financial forecast covering the coming three to five years (depending on the timeframe of your business plan). Any market expansion opportunities (including M&A) should be outlined and risks summarized.

At this point, you should have the framework of the business plan. It should clearly stake out the boundaries of the business as well as the strategic assets and core capabilities that will ensure a disciplined focus on the priorities. It should explain relevant market and customer dynamics, the competitive landscape, the firm's positioning, and its sources of competitive advantage.

It's Still About Progress, not Perfection

A business plan is, first and foremost, a strategic plan that builds on the strategic framework that has been created and embodies the management team's vision for success. Think of it as a vision for where and how the company will win both in the coming year and in the longer term. The dimensions of the win include customer, product, and operational effectiveness. The question that must be answered about this future is this: *What will be our position in the competitive marketplace?*

No vision of the future is perfect. It can be improved as it is reality-tested through time in the real world, but within the brief compass of the first hundred days, the purpose of the vision is to get the organization moving in the right direction, positioned to earn the right to grow. A bias for action always drives the first hundred days.

The *what* should be followed by a *where,* which defines the company's strategic customers (A customers) in the near and long term, and a *how*, which is an aspect of the strategy aimed at uniquely satisfying the company's A customers. The strategy must create a sustainable competitive advantage for at least whatever timeline management has defined as "long term." In the real world, the strategy's success can be determined by whether it has carried the company to or beyond the goal defined in step 1.

Business plans come in all shapes and sizes but tend to share a common table of contents. For a business requiring turnaround, begin with the goal from step 1 and a mission statement that states *how* and *where* the company will win in the marketplace.

Next, enumerate the *major changes from last year*. You can't know where you are going if you don't know where you are, and you can't know where you are if you don't know where you were. The plan should highlight the most significant changes at the company, important changes in the marketplace, important changes in technology, and impactful changes in the competitive environment. Emphasis should be put on the changes that will affect the business going forward. To the extent possible, all changes should be defined in numbers—dollars, quantities, and percentages.

A *situation analysis* follows. This takes a self-critical approach in delivering the facts about the current and historical state of the business, emphasizing where the company is winning—and where it is not. The situation analysis should be meaningfully granular. For instance, the business may be broken down by major product lines. Growth and profitability should be broken down by product. A products should be identified and highlighted.

Other breakdowns might include performance analysis by state, region, or country. Sales analysis may be segmented by channel. Also potentially important are analyses of relevant trends in technology, markets in terms of market size and growth, segmentation by product type and customer, and competitor market shares. Likely, strategies should conclude the market analysis.

In the context of the three- or five-year goal (step 1), restate or formulate three to five high-priority objectives, which may be related to any or all of the following:

1. Customer segments to be penetrated
2. Products to be developed
3. Channels to access to reach the customer segments identified
4. Operational effectiveness
5. Data required

With these final five pieces of information, the business plan is sufficiently complete to *launch the action plan* (step 4).

CHAPTER 9

Step 4: Action Plan

⬡ ⬡ ⬡

"For the things we have to learn before we can do them, we learn by doing them."

—ARISTOTLE, Nicomachean Ethics, ca. 300 BC, book II, chapter 1

IN THE FIRST hundred days, the fourth and final step is drafting and implementing an *action plan*, which defines the imperatives and tactics necessary to execute the strategy (step 2) within the 80/20 segmented structure outlined in step 3. Like the three steps that precede it, step 4 aims for progress (not perfection) toward delivering on the goal (step 1). Every day of the first hundred days is dedicated to making sound, informed decisions and acting based on them. However imperfect, action injects the company strategy into the real world, where it not only can begin the needed turnaround but is also tested against reality to continuously improve it.

Who, What, and When?

A business plan is no more than an inert plan until it is implemented. *Action* is not an idea or a description. It is an event that requires doers who do specific things at specific times. A successful action plan seamlessly connects the business plan *strategy* to the *life* of the business by assigning the *who, what*, and *when* that are instrumental in converting the plan into action.

1. The *who* consists of those with direct leadership and operational responsibility for implementing each aspect of the business plan. Clearly, assigning the *who* is critical because a plan is nothing but an abstraction until human beings act on it. The *who* aspect of the business plan has important implications for internal HR (promotions, transfers, relocations, etc.) and possible talent acquisition from outside the company.

2. Each *what* must be a clear definition of an action or set of actions and should include whatever resources are required to perform the action(s).

3. Each *when* must be specified with dates. This means that the business plan needs to embody realistic and realistically coordinated scheduling.

In sum, an action plan includes human resources, finance, and logistics issues, which need to be resolved within a sufficiently detailed and explicit plan to ensure that each of the three *Ws* is feasible—that is, capable of successful execution likely to produce profitable growth.

Launched

Within the first hundred days, your business plan (step 3) is a work in progress but is far enough advanced to require an action plan (step 4) to lay out its execution. The action plan will be launched after the first one hundred days. It, too, will be far from perfect at this early stage, but it will be good enough to define key tactics and the efforts required to execute that other work in progress, the business plan (step 3).

During the first hundred days, block out a high-level action plan, which should specify the principal actions to advance you toward the goal in step 1. As far as possible, the high-level plan should then be fleshed out, breaking down the high-level elements into multiple specific tasks. The secret to creating an effective action plan is blatantly obvious: *Think in terms of* actions.

1. ***Recap the goal defined in the business plan.*** This step reinforces the context for the actions to be defined. Goals are the desired endpoints of the strategy set out in the business plan. Goals are the products of strategy.

2. ***Recap the objectives defined in the business plan.*** "Goals" and "objectives" are not synonyms. Goals are desired endpoints, whereas objectives are milestones and intermediate deliverables toward that endpoint. Goals are made up of objectives and achieved when all those objectives are successfully attained. Defining objectives is necessarily more granular and specific than outlining goals.

3. ***Define and lay out the action steps (the "projects") to achieve each goal outlined in the business plan.*** Each action step (often called a "project") is a set of related tasks ("action items") that must be successfully executed to produce the deliverables. Together, these deliverables make up the goals set out in the business plan. It will not be possible to lay out all of these in the first one hundred days.

4. ***Identify and prioritize all necessary action items.*** Action steps ("projects") typically consist of a sequence of smaller tasks, which may be called "action items." Breaking them out and prioritizing them provides a clear set of instructions for successfully completing each action step. Typically, action items must or should be performed in an optimal sequence. This requires identifying which action items depend on completing other action items. Identifying all such dependencies puts a *when* to the *what*. At the very least, the sequencing by dependencies increases efficiency and allows for coordination of effort

among the team. In "Toyota Way" terms, this minimizes *muda* (waste). It is at step 4 that laying out a graphical timeline of action steps and items can be most helpful. The graphical representation of actions through time simplifies project management and promotes accountability in ways essential to lean management. Again, it will not be possible to lay out all of these in the action plan as it exists in the first one hundred days.

5. ***Define roles and responsibilities.*** Having defined, divided, and subdivided the work required to execute the action plan, the next step is to define the *who*. It is now time to assign ownership of each action step ("project") and item that makes up the action step. Those assigned ownership for whole projects or individual action items must fully understand their roles and responsibilities. Step 5 is the place to define and assign these. Tasks should be assigned as far as possible in the action plan as it exists at the end of the first one hundred days. These roles and responsibilities will doubtless change somewhat during the three to five years to which the business plan applies.

6. ***Allocate resources.*** Step 5 allocates management resources to the projects and action items that comprise the action plan. Step 6 includes management personnel but goes beyond them to allocate additional human resources required for each action step ("project") and item. Other resources may include funding, equipment, physical plant, materials, advanced computing time, outside consultants, workspace, special certifications or licenses, etc. Resource allocation must be made in the context of the entire business plan. Failing to do this results in suboptimization—inadequate or inefficient resource allocation—a major source of waste (*muda*). Get as far in this task as possible by the end of the first

one hundred days, knowing that the allocation is subject to modification as realities of the moment may require.

7. ***Apply the SMART standard to objectives.*** The action plan requires close monitoring and continuous feedback on performance (see *do, check,* and *act* below). It is a mistake to rely on subjective assessments, gut feelings, and hunches in assessing progress toward goals. In 1911, Frederick Taylor stressed the importance of measuring what you monitor and using the resulting empirical data to find the best ways to run each production process. This was the cornerstone of his concept of scientific management. Today, this quantified, objective approach is often identified by the acronym "SMART": *specific, measurable, assignable, realistic,* and *time-related*. All action steps and items should embody these qualities, and their progress should be evaluated according to them. Evaluate each goal and deliverable in SMART terms so that you can be assured of accurately evaluating progress toward your business goals.

8. ***Allocate time.*** Each project requires time, and allocating it requires a timeline. Break down action steps into action items and provide reasonable (parallel where possible, sequential where necessary) deadlines for each.

SMART Goals

SMART goals *are specific, measurable, assignable, realistic,* and *time-related*, which means that progress toward their realization can be evaluated meaningfully. This step in the action plan is an important opportunity for assessing and, if necessary, revising or refining business plan goals. If, in formulating the action plan, you discover that a goal is not SMART—that it cannot be assessed objectively and with measurable data—it is important to modify that goal to make it SMART.

Is the goal specific? That is, who will be involved in achieving it? What resources will be required? Why is the goal important?

Is the goal measurable? "What gets measured gets done" is a pronouncement often attributed to management guru Peter Drucker. He may or may not have said this, but he could have, and he should have. People must know where they are going and how far they have gotten. Purpose and motivation are tightly bound to measurement. While people debate the origin of the quotation attributed to Drucker, they are sure that Yogi Berra said, "If you don't know where you are going, you might wind up someplace else." For major goals, it is helpful to create project milestones to further aid in measurement and direction.

Is the goal assignable? Can the actions necessary to achieve the goal be assigned to managers and employees capable of carrying out the action steps? Does the organization have people who can do what needs to be done? If not, can these people be found?

Is the goal realistic? The poet Robert Browning famously wrote, "A man's reach should exceed his grasp, or what's a heaven for?" That is a noble sentiment, but there is no point in setting and measuring an unrealistic goal. Always assess feasibility.

Is the goal time-related? The goal must not be open-ended but bound to time with the taut cords of a deadline. Deadlines should be evaluated for feasibility, but they must exist. Time is a measurable dimension that must be measured. Without deadlines, coordination of multiple tasks is impossible, and motivation is made much more difficult than it needs to be.

Act

The aim of the first hundred days is to begin taking positive action to earn the right to grow. In a turnaround, the sooner you start turning, the better. You cannot afford to wait for perfection. The action plan will inform sound decisions to drive the organization forward into the real world. The effects of the interaction between the strategy and its implementation in the real world must be monitored, and the results must be fed back into the ongoing execution. Based on the resulting data, you can make changes to move the imperfect strategy closer to perfection.

Immediately engage a *do, check, act* process to ensure adequate and accurate feedback to monitor the progress of the action plan and take corrective measures as needed:

> ***Do:*** Execute the plan—implement the countermeasures—and collect data on results.
>
> ***Check:*** Evaluate the results produced by implementing the countermeasures. Assess the execution of the plan. Your objective is to verify your hypothesis for the countermeasure and evaluate the timeliness of realizing the benefit. Above all, learn from the result to improve the team's problem-solving capabilities. What worked? What did not work? And why?
>
> ***Act:*** Determine the next steps in executing the business strategy or plan through continuous improvement. Based on the results—degree of improvement or decline—decide what to do next. For successful countermeasures, disseminate them to other processes or areas. For countermeasures that fail to produce change or create decline, continue collecting results and reevaluate the nature and status of the problem or issue.

Use an Action Plan Template and/or Software

Create or use a readymade action plan template to collect, collate, and track tasks, assignments, and deadlines. Here is a sample of a very basic action plan template:

Benchmarks for Success	Evaluation Plan	Strategic Action Descriptions	Party / Dept Responsible	Date to Begin	Date Due	Resources Required	Potential Hazards	Desired Outcomes					Additional Notes

Fig. 09-01: A basic action plan template.

A good deal of project management software is available, which might not do much of the heavy lifting for you—thinking is required—but can take over a good deal of the mundane drudgery. Offerings, prices, and product evaluations change frequently, so your best option is to fire up your browser and type in "project management software."

Iterate as Needed

No business plan is carved in stone. The action plan has two purposes. The first is to convert the business plan from potential energy into kinetic energy. The second is to audit it to ensure this conversion is feasible and modifiable to accommodate changing realities. As the *do, check, act* process progresses, modify the action plan as necessary to better support the budget and the execution of the strategy. Review, edit, elaborate, and refine the complete enumeration of the risks and opportunities for the business.

PART III

Beyond the First Hundred Days:

The PGOS Management Practice

Portfolio

CHAPTER 10

Strategy

● ● ●

*"If you can't explain what you're doing in simple English,
you are probably doing something wrong."*

—ALFRED KAHN, *Time Magazine* (May 8, 1978)

IN PART II of this book, we laid out the process for creating and acting on a hundred-day strategy for positioning the company to earn the right to grow. After those first hundred days, the strategy must be amplified and expanded for the long term, guiding three to five years of profitable growth. During these three to five years, the strategy is reformulated annually. Each annual iteration may introduce course corrections and other changes, ranging from minor adjustments to major realignments.

Recall from part II that the first step in the first hundred days is to set a goal. This identifies *what* needs to be done. The second step, creating the strategy, is *how* to reach the goal. During the first hundred days, the short-term purpose of step 2, creating the strategy, is simply to get the company to step 3, in which the executive and operational leadership puts some meat on step 2's strategic bones and gives the business a new structure going forward. This structure aims to accelerate the application of 80/20 by optimizing focus on the most productive segment of the company's customer base and product offerings, thereby driving profitable growth.

In effect, the first hundred days iteration of the strategy is nothing more or less than a working model. In some manufacturing businesses, an important early step beyond building a single prototype is creating an "MVP," a minimum viable product that can be released to the market to test its viability and elicit consumer response, or as Eric Ries says in his *Lean Startup* (Crown Currency, 2011), "that version of a new product which allows a team to collect the maximum amount of validated learning about customers with the least effort." The strategy of the first hundred days is the MVP iteration of the strategy. With those hundred days in the rearview mirror, it is time to build a full-scale, fully featured strategy for the long term. This iteration defines how you intend to profitably grow the business in current and potential markets. A strategy to grow profitably is establishing, creating, and maintaining a competitive advantage in all its chosen markets.

Critical Functions of the Strategy

The long-term strategy guides profitable growth that will create value *above* the expectations of all stakeholders, including shareholders, customers, employees, vendors, and the community in which the business operates. It also includes competitors. A successful strategy will produce value exceeding even *their* expectations—much to their chagrin.

A competent strategy guides four critical choices:

1. Where to compete
2. How to compete
3. The actions that must be taken to execute the strategy
4. The investments and allocations of resources required to execute the strategy

The strategy is not a secret document. It is a five-year Constitution, subject to yearly amendment, and it is meant to be central to the organization and shared by its leadership. It is the product of collaboration among the company's leaders and thus represents the shared senior view of how the company will earn the right to grow and win in the marketplace.

The Strategic Process

The process behind the long-term strategy is a more detailed iteration of the process behind the hundred-day strategy. The essence is the same, but the effect expands in time and space. The long-term strategy builds on the same three steps that apply to the first hundred days:

1. Situation assessment
2. Strategic framework
3. Business plan

What assumes significantly greater importance in the three- to five-year iteration of the strategy are the following:

1. A feedback loop (policy deployment), perhaps formalized as a monthly business review
2. The application of enterprise risk deployment

It is only natural that these two elements would assume greater significance in the long-term strategy because they operate in time. Only after the strategy has been in execution for some period does it produce measurable outcomes. This data must be continuously monitored and analyzed, with quarterly reviews and a major evaluation and assessment at the end of each year. The tracked feedback are the key performance indicators (KPIs), which provide quantified measures revealing whether the current strategy is producing the desired outcomes. Grumbling about reports is a favorite participator sport in virtually every business organization. And it is certainly true that many businesses do a lot of measuring, which can be maddening.

There is some dispute over whether management guru Peter Drucker actually said, "What gets measured gets done," "What gets measured gets improved," or "What gets measured gets managed." However, all three versions are easily misread and would benefit from the addition of a final clause:

> "What gets measured gets done *if you measure strictly with the intention of doing.*"
> "What gets measured gets improved *if you measure strictly with the intention of improving,*"
> "What gets measured gets managed *if you measure strictly with the intention of managing,*"

The problem is that too many businesses measure only with the intention of reporting the measurements. Reporting is not a reason to measure. The reason to measure *is* to do, improve, manage, or undertake all three.

Managing Risk

Managing risk is so essential that it needs to start in the first hundred days. At that point, it is mainly a predictive and speculative exercise—an attempt to forecast the weather, looking for storms, droughts, and conditions that may produce fire. During the three to five years in which a long-term strategy is deployed, risk management is an ongoing management function. Chapter 11 lays out risk management in detail, including the advanced enterprise risk management (ERM) method. ERM is applied at every step of the strategic process to identify potential risks and opportunities in the unfolding strategy. ERM triggers and informs additional planning throughout the ongoing development and improvement of the strategy.

The Divergent/Convergent Strategic Cycle

Chapters 3 and 8 discuss in detail divergent and convergent thinking, so I will not repeat the full discussion here. But do take note of the three diamond-shaped symbols in the illustration of the strategic management process in this chapter (figure 10-01). The shape is purposeful because the three phases of the strategic process begin with divergent thinking and conclude with convergent thinking.

Here's why: Thinking strategically requires that all potentially relevant issues, problems, solutions, and opportunities be identified and inventoried—that nothing important be missed or prematurely excluded. Yet thinking strategically also requires the strategists to come to definite conclusions in the form of action items enumerated in an action plan. Therefore, each of the three steps must begin with divergent thinking (inclusive) and conclude with convergent thinking (thinking that filters down to the most critical actions). The strategists must discipline themselves to exercise divergent and convergent thinking sequentially and in strict order. Only this kind of discipline is likely to facilitate truly strategic decisions. Contaminate divergence with convergence, and the strategists are bound to overlook something potentially important. Contaminate convergence with divergence, and the strategists will waste valuable time or perhaps fail to reach actionable conclusions. In this way, as Shakespeare's Hamlet put it, even "enterprises of great pith and moment... lose the name of action" and are drowned in the "pale cast of thought."

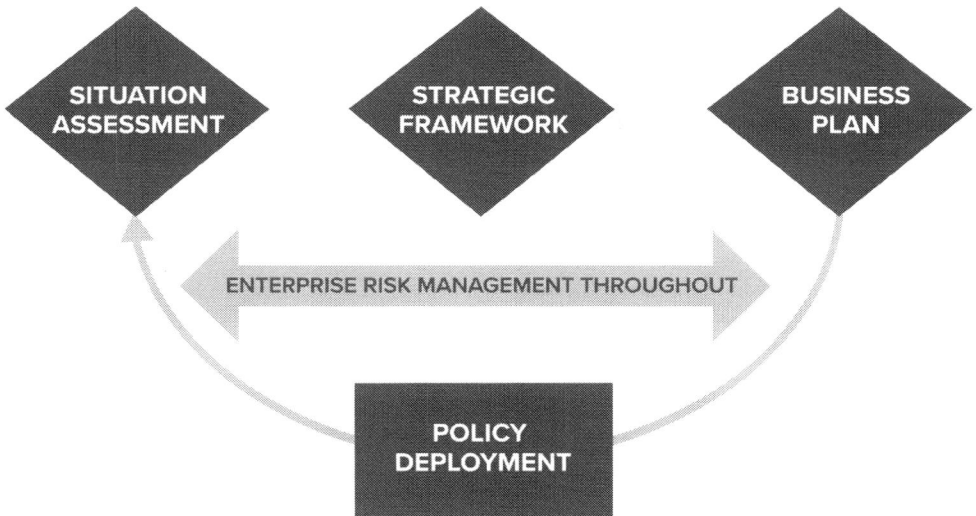

Fig 10-01: The strategy process.

The angle on the left side of each diamond widens outward, representing the phase of divergent thinking, while the angle on the right side represents convergent thinking, in which the divergent harvest of thought is reaped and winnowed into specific insights, absolute direction, and feasible strategic actions.

The cycle of the strategic process spans the full calendar year, with timeframes to keep it on track. At the end of the year, the resulting strategy has been revised and improved. Yet, it too will be the subject of review and revision in the following year—and so on, until the end of the three- or five-year strategic cycle is reached. Each year, the divergent/convergent discipline is applied to make revisions. In this way, the strategy is never allowed to become the frozen letter of Holy Writ but, rather, the agile product of continuous learning.

Strategy Management Process

The entire strategy management process encompasses the situation assessment, the strategic framework, and the business plan.

Situation Assessment

The situation assessment asks and answers a series of questions in five categories.

1. **Business analysis.** What were the strategic priorities of the prior year? What can be learned from these? What does the historical record of growth and profitability reveal? Historically, what have been the company's strengths, weaknesses, opportunities, and threats (SWOT analysis)? Historically, what are the company's core complacencies and strategic assets (CCSA)? Did the business meet stakeholder expectations in the prior year?

2. **Customers.** Who are the company's customers? What do they want? Where do they want to get it? Are they getting it from our company? If not, from where else? How are the needs of our customers changing? How can our company change to meet these needs and serve our customers profitably?

3. **Portfolio.** How is the company's portfolio (of products/services and/or of component companies and divisions) performing in profitable growth? How do we optimize the current portfolio? What should our future portfolio look like? What is required to improve our portfolio?

4. **Markets.** What markets does the company serve? What are the key trends and drivers? How attractive are the markets the company currently serves? How is attractiveness changing? What accounts for changes in the company's current markets? Should we consider new markets?

5. **Competitors.** What is the basis of the company's competition? Quality? Service? Price? How intense is the competition? How is the competition changing? How is the competition positioned versus our company? How does our company compare with the competition on key customer value metrics? How can we establish, obtain, or sustain a superior competitive position?

6. **Timing.** Allotting the first six months of the year (calendar or fiscal) to the situation assessment is best. The kickoff meeting takes place in the first month, with two check-in meetings in months four and five. The purpose of these meetings is to present progress on the situation assessment. During the final month of the situation assessment process, a workshop is held to identify and work on lessons learned. The workshop may span one to two days. At the end of the final month, the assessment team reports to the executive management team.

7. **Outputs.** The team responsible for the situation assessment should create a year-end summary of key insights, with supporting data and analysis that reveal these as the critical focal points for the strategic framework. A full report is submitted yearly to the executive management team.

Strategic Framework

The second step in the strategy process, the strategic framework, takes the insights from the situation assessment and generates key strategic goals and initiatives. The process typically spans two months, confirming and reaffirming the current strategy or crafting revisions as its objective.

The strategic framework supplies the answers to the following:

1. What is required to achieve breakthrough growth and performance?
2. What differentiators are required to win?
3. What are the key strategic issues?
4. What are the key strategic opportunities?
5. What are the highest-value, highest-priority (80/20) opportunities?
6. What are the critical few (80/20) initiatives?

Divergent thinking should be applied to identify opportunities and issues, especially in the following areas:

1. New market and product development
2. Adjacencies
3. Acquisitions and divestiture
4. Network/footprint
5. Make/buy
6. New capabilities
7. Core business improvement
8. Market attractiveness improvement
9. Competitive position improvement

Convergent thinking is next applied to the output from the divergent phase to develop the critical few (80/20) opportunities and initiatives. The objective is to analyze trade-offs between options and identify those likely to produce the highest shareholder or stakeholder value.

In selecting the highest-value issues or opportunities, the strategists must consider:

1. Potential
2. Affordability
3. Execution ease

4. Identification of core competencies and strategic assets (CCSA) to be leveraged or created
5. Relatedness to the CCSAs

To develop the critical few strategic initiatives relating most closely to the strategy, the following should be identified or addressed:

1. Three to five key initiatives
2. The critical changes needed to execute the initiatives
3. Financial analysis and projections
4. Resources required
5. Risk assessments for each initiative
6. High-level action plan for each initiative
7. Milestones should be specified for each initiative.

Timing. This phase typically requires about ninety days. It begins just as the situation assessment is concluded, the one process handing off the work to the other. It consists of a kickoff meeting and a check-in meeting to review the insights and lessons learned from the situation analysis. Shortly after this, a workshop (one or two days) creates the strategic framework, reported after the typically allotted ninety days.

Outputs of the strategic framework team include a summary of where the company will compete, how it will compete, what capabilities are required to compete, and why the company will win. This framework output must include

1. Mission and vision
2. Prior-year strategy overview
3. Business environment assessment
4. Strategic priorities summary
5. Strategic objectives

6. Definition/scoping and rationale
7. Value-at-risk/value-creation potential
8. Strategic priority detail for three to five strategic initiatives
9. Key programs/projects, actions, resources, organizational implications, and investments to execute the strategic priorities
10. A three- to five-year strategic financial forecast
11. Strategic initiative Gantt charts, with hypothesis, high-level timing, and resource requirements
12. Market expansion opportunities (M&A), if appropriate
13. Risks summary with heat map templates
14. Critical success factors

At the end of its work, the framework team reports to the executive management team.

Business Plan

The third step of the strategy process is the business plan, which uses the strategic initiatives delineated in the strategic framework to guide an action plan. This is a bottom-up plan responsive to the performance measured throughout the year. It includes detailed financials.

The business plan is developed in a series of meetings over ninety days, which produce a financial forecast and a plan to execute the strategic initiatives and business strategy defined in the strategic framework. The business plan articulates the steps necessary to accomplish the strategic objectives described in the strategic framework. It also serves to forecast the strategy's expected financial results and determine how best to allocate resources to deliver the forecasted results.

Four major questions must be answered in the business plan:

1. What is the budget?
2. What is the action plan?
3. What are the significant risks associated with the strategy, and how are these addressed?
4. Are the right organizational measures and processes present to execute the strategy?

The business plan is what puts the strategic framework into action, yet even it starts with divergent thinking. This is the time to analyze the output from the strategic framework phase, including vision, mission, objectives, and initiatives. The divergent approach looks for and considers alternative actions and options for achieving the strategy. The strategists must identify all the tangible steps required to translate strategy into specific actions.

Considering the alternatives and the associated steps, the strategists shift from divergent to convergent thinking to prioritize the most important actions (including alternative ones) and use these to formulate milestones and deliverables to output a detailed action plan.

The budget for the coming year is based on the action plan and functional plans to support the strategy and meet the specified budget. This is also the time and place to ensure that all critical risks are managed, with a risk-management plan agreed upon.

Outputs. The business plan consists of a high-level strategy-at-a-glance, with an X-matrix to help ensure alignment of the strategic objectives, KPIs, and the action components of the plan. This summary should include:

1. Linkage to both the situation assessment and strategic framework
2. Strategic objectives
3. Three to five strategic initiatives, along with associated verification metrics

In addition, the business plan lays out the action plans for each strategic initiative to include

1. Hypothesis
2. Leader
3. Learning
4. Why the initiative will win for the company
5. Gantt chart
6. Expected results, with KPIs

Finally, the business plan includes a detailed strategic plan for the coming year, specifying:

1. Budget with detailed functional budgets
2. Detailed income statement
3. KPIs with financial goals
4. Capital expenditure
5. Working capital
6. Investment leverage (IL)
7. Talent acquisition and development plan
8. Headcount plan
9. Critical risks and opportunities
10. Mergers and acquisitions plan, if applicable
11. Three- to five-year high-level financial plan

Strategy in Action

How often have you heard something like this: "It was a great strategy. Too bad the execution failed"? Done right, creating a great strategy makes it impossible to divide strategy from execution and execution from strategy. The PGOS approach to strategy makes the action plan integral to the business plan and makes the business plan integral to the strategy via the strategic framework. To qualify as competent, let alone great, a strategy must contain within it the means of its successful execution. This is the aim of the PGOS approach.

CHAPTER 11

80/20 Segment and Focus

◈ ◈ ◈

"Everything should be made as simple as possible, but not simpler."

—ALBERT EINSTEIN, quoted in *Reader's Digest,* July 1977

THE MOST POWERFUL tool in the 80/20 toolkit is simplification, a process for focusing a business through segmentation. To reduce complexity in areas most important to the business, simplification may require reducing the number of products or models in a product line and/or the number and type of customers the sales organization is focused on reaching.

Who is the seminal authority on simplification in business? Frederick Winslow Taylor merits a deep bow, but most would nominate Peter Drucker. Of all his remarkably influential management ideas, none is more important than Drucker's conviction that companies tend to produce too many products in too great variety, that they hire employees they don't need, and that they expand into markets and economic sectors they would be far better off avoiding.

Well, no one ever got fired for reading—or quoting—Peter Drucker, but I prefer an earlier source, earlier than either Taylor or Drucker. Henry David Thoreau was born in Concord, Massachusetts, in 1817 and died forty-four years later. He could have taken over his father's prosperous and innovative pencil-making business, but the work didn't suit him, so he became a naturalist, environmentalist, philosopher, political activist, and essayist. He built a small house—today, it would be called a "tiny house"—on land his friend and mentor Ralph Waldo Emerson gave him in a second-growth forest on the shore of Walden Pond, Massachusetts, and moved into it on July 4, 1845. There, he wrote two books and made notes for a third, *Walden*, published in 1854 and read by almost no one at the time. About a century after he died, *Walden* became so widely read and admired that the twentieth-century poet Robert Frost called it the "one book [that] surpasses everything we have had in America."

In the second chapter of *Walden*, titled "Where I Lived, and What I Lived For," Thoreau explained why he built a little house in the woods and went to live there:

> I went to the woods because I wished to live deliberately, to front only the essential facts of life, and see if I could not learn what it had to teach, and not, when I came to die, discover that I had not lived. I did not wish to live what was not life, living is so dear; nor did I wish to practice resignation, unless it was quite necessary. I wanted to live deep and suck out all the marrow of life, to live so sturdily and Spartan-like as to put to rout all that was not life, to cut a broad swath and shave close, to drive life into a corner, and reduce it to its lowest terms, and, if it proved to be mean, why then to get the whole and genuine meanness of it, and publish its meanness to the world; or if it were sublime, to know it by experience, and be able to give a true account of it in my next excursion.

Now *that* is what I call simplification. A lot of people admire this passage, but few have been able to take it to heart and live their lives according to the pattern Thoreau sets out in it. That's understandable. After all, becoming something like a monk, hermit, or Zen master isn't for everyone, but anyone who owns, leads, or manages a business can learn a lot from these few words.

For CEOs and managers, the takeaway lessons from *Walden* include the following: Run your business *deliberately*. Identify, grapple with, and leverage *only the essential facts*. Invest the organization's assets, time, and effort only in what is productive and not in what is unproductive or even less than optimally productive. Why? Because those assets, time, and effort are "so dear" that you cannot afford to squander them.

Run your business to make the very most of it all the time. Deploy 80 percent of your resources to "suck out all the marrow" (the *critical few*), putting "to rout all that" constitutes the *trivial many*. Use your strategy to "cut a broad swath and shave close," reducing the objects of your time, effort, and cash to their "lowest terms."

This chapter details the tactics and tools a business can employ to "shave close," simplifying the number of products and volume of customers, paring these down to the roughly 20 percent that generates roughly 80 percent of your revenue. But while eliminating products is a prime simplification approach, it is obviously subject to the law of diminishing returns. This chapter will detail "the Dirty Dozen," a suite of alternative tactics aimed at maximizing the performance even of B products and B customers.

Analyzing for Segmentation

Earlier in this book, we discussed how analyzing the data generated by your customers, products, sales, costs, profitability, markets, and regions can be used to "segment" your product/customer revenue into quads that reveal the performance of (1) your A products/A customers, (2) B products/A customers, (3) A products/B customers, and (4) your B products/B customers.

By using 80/20 to generate the quads, you segment your product/customer combinations and thereby reveal what combinations are generating roughly 80 percent of your revenue and significantly more than 80 percent of profits. To this segment—segment number 1, your A products/A customers (roughly 20 percent)—you should be allocating as close to 80 percent of your assets and effort as you can. The remaining three quadrants must be addressed proportionally:

- Quadrant 1 is often called "the Fort" and merits approximately 80 percent of the company's resources.
- Quadrant 2 is regarded as the "necessary evil." Since the B products in this quadrant are bought by A customers, providing just the right level of resources to serve this combination is necessary to keep those A customers happy, even if that means minimal profit or break-even performance.
- Quadrant 3 products/customers consist of products purchased by B customers. These are considered good business if run only transactionally, using the fewest possible resources. This quadrant may well be a significant source of opportunistic profit.
- Quadrant 4 products/customers typically represent a small fraction of revenue and, also typically, a loss—negative profit. The solution is to price these products up, simplify and automate the selling process, and drop the products that create nothing but loss. This means letting the lowest-performing customers go and, in short, exiting this market.

Act on the Analysis by Simplifying

The most potent tool you have for acting upon the segmentation analysis is simplification. Reduce complexity in areas that are most important to the business. The most direct way of doing this is to reduce product offerings and/or the number of models or variations of products offered. Simplifying the product line will likely result in the loss of some customers. But, applying 80/20, you may decide that your sales team should not focus on B customers except for those who buy A products.

In 2014, McDonald's suffered both declining sales and falling stock valuations. One of the company's approaches to reviving its business was simplifying its menu. As The Motley Fool website reported (December 16, 2014), "In monthly sales reports and quarterly earnings releases, Chief Executive Officer Don Thompson repeatedly cited the complicated menu as a problem, and vowed to fix it, without offering much in the way of specifics. That is, until now. McDonald's is finally doing something to simplify its one hundred-plus-item menu, eliminating five Extra Value Meals and eight items that could include variations of the Quarter Pounder with Cheese, Premium Chicken sandwich, and Snack Wrap." Common sense almost always drives a "bigger is better" approach, but McDonald's discovered that putting more on the menu is not the fast lane to higher sales and profits. Customers were so overwhelmed by choices that it took them longer to place orders and workers longer to complete the orders. This resulted in bottlenecks at the counter and the drive-up window and dissatisfied customers who, let's not forget, were there for *fast* food.

McDonald's refocused on offering "80s" items—the meals most customers wanted most of the time—and delivering what customers also valued highly: time-saving speed.

For products in quadrant 4, you will want to price up to the point that these B products selling to B customers become profitable. Almost certainly, at least some B customers in this quadrant will leave you. Quadrant 4 sales should be made with minimum resource commitment from the sales force. This is also true for quadrant 3—A products purchased by B customers—but the A customers purchasing B products in quadrant 2 expect some degree of sales force commitment and should receive it.

What I have just said is intended as a rule of thumb. Base your allocation of resources on *your* unique analysis of *your* unique data. It will almost certainly simplify your decision-making by looking at the balancing act this way: You want guidelines that will *prevent* you and your organization from working to improve parts of the business incapable of making or unlikely to make a significant positive impact on the business. No sense in devoting anything like 80 percent of your resources to serving customers who account for a modest fraction of revenue and profit. Serving these B customers with the same level of service allocated to your A customers is a loss to the business. You literally cannot afford this lack of segmentation.

Choose Your Tool

At the risk of becoming repetitious, the simplest tool to choose for simplification is to simplify the number of products the business offers. The A products in quadrants 1 and 2 are likely immune from simplification, but a large number of products—roughly 80 percent—that produce just 20 percent of your total revenue are candidates for the simplest form of simplification. Because they create unnecessary complexity that bleeds resources away from the A products, cutting the worst-performing B products from your inventory reduces losses and voracious opportunity costs by freeing up resources to serve the A product/A customer quadrant.

If you thoughtlessly devote maximum resources to unprofitable products and product lines, you will cannibalize the company's performance regarding your best products and customers.

The Dirty Dozen

In the Dirty Dozen simplification toolbox, the just-get-rid-of-it approach is called "No Scrubs," which purges all B products that offer no strategic advantage. But this is just one of the simplification approaches the Dirty Dozen offers. The first four relate directly to customers:

1. **Can't Buy Me Love:** Stop offering discounts to B customers, especially on B products.
2. **Money for Nothing:** Stop paying sales commissions on B customer business.
3. **Money (That's What I Want):** Require credit card payment upfront with a fee.
4. **All the Small Things:** Set a minimum-order value/quantity. Minimum line value/quantity. Make the sale worth your while.

The next eight relate to products:

1. **Circle of Life:** Substitute 80's products from a preferred vendor.
2. **No Scrubs:** Drop B products that have no strategic value. These losers are killing you.
3. **Ain't No Mountain High Enough:** Price the product up. Customers can have it—but it will cost them!
4. **Take It or Leave It:** Offer the product in a standard/single package size. Do not break bulk. Take it or leave it.
5. **Time After Time:** Aggregate orders until fulfillment

makes sense for you. The customer can buy it, but it will take time.

6. **Don't You (Forget About Me):** Specify scheduled days for service or order. Stop firefighting for unprofitable business.

7. **My Way:** Offer a few standard option packages instead of a mix-and-match buffet of options.

8. **You've Got Another Thing Coming:** Offer only the complete package and let the customer discard what they don't need. That is, consolidate into one full-featured product.

But there are important alternatives to consider before you lead with what is the nuclear option. *Pricing* is easy and quite effective at reducing the risk of maintaining a product or product line at a loss. "Ain't No Mountain High Enough" simply demands a high price. If you have a cadre of customers who really do need a certain B product, by all means, offer it to them—but offer it at whatever price these customers, holding their noses, will pay in preference to not being able to obtain the product at all. It's either pay up or walk the plank.

"Don't You (Forget About Me)" is a more complicated tool but is useful for marginally performing products that are sold to marginally productive customers. Make specials or low-volume runs on preannounced dates only. This will concentrate demand and therefore concentrate (and thus limit) the need for resources. It will also improve cash flow by concentrating the conversion to sales of some B-product offerings.

Another way of managing costs in selling B products to mostly B customers is the "Time After Time" approach, in which you pool sufficient orders of a product to make a special or low-volume order large enough to run profitably. In other words, you do not sell product X until you have booked sufficient orders to make the sale worthwhile.

Simplifying a product need not inevitably mean eliminating it. Offer it as "My Way" only. Keep the item but reduce the variety of sizes or options.

Upselling is a tried-and-true tactic for increasing the margin on certain products. For some B products, you can make the upsell effectively mandatory with "You've Got Another Thing Coming." Include all possible components or accessories associated with the product in question so that, to acquire the item, customers must buy a bundle or set. Customers pay for the complete package, which they can tailor to their needs by discarding what they don't want. Many budget restaurants save production costs by adhering to a "no substitutions" policy. This approach rules out à la carte as an option.

Segment the Business Itself

Customers and products are both subject to segmentation. And so is the business itself. You may discover that your business has evolved or grown to the point that it has become a collection of dissimilar businesses. If the aggregated businesses are very significantly dissimilar, 80/20 applied to products and customers and product/customer quads may not be sufficient to simplify your allocation of resources effectively. In this case, consider separating unlike businesses into smaller businesses that can better focus on more specialized areas. The benefit is that you will be able to track each specialized business more easily and accurately and tailor dedicated resources to the needs of customer bases with similar needs. Segmenting the business can be an alternative to simply discontinuing product lines that underperform because they are not getting sufficient attention from the resources available in a larger, unsegmented business.

Let's say you have a business that sells capital-intensive products, such as large machinery, and also offers the associated parts and services. While these are certainly related businesses, they might benefit from employing entirely different marketing, sales, distribution, and service approaches. The first step in segmenting such a business is to perform separate quad segmentation for the capital products and the parts and services offerings. Segmenting the proposed two businesses by quadrants will help you create well-defined and separate P&Ls around each business and its newly recognized segments.

Product type is not the only way to segment a business. Some businesses may be segmented by customer types, market segments, or international geographies. But how can you determine if segmenting the business would be a useful strategy for your organization? Creating and analyzing quads for each proposed business is a good start and will enable you to create meaningful P&Ls for the different entities. It is also important, however, to begin by developing a 360-degree view and deep understanding of the company as it presently exists and operates. Here are the questions to ask and answer:

UNDERSTAND THE COMPANY BEFORE DECIDING ON SEGMENTATION
Mission, Vision, Values

1. Review the mission, vision, and values.
2. What is the history behind the organization's vision, mission, and values?
3. Have these been adopted throughout the organization?
4. How are the mission, vision, and values visible in everyday work?
5. How do colleagues express their values?

Objectives, Goals, Strategy, Metrics

1. What is the company's operating model?
2. What are the objectives, strategy, metrics, and operating plans?
3. How does the company use metrics to run the business?
4. What annual strategic planning process does it use?

Business Segments, Divisions, Regions, Functions, Distributors

1. How do the strategies and activities of each function, region, department, and distributor support the corporate strategy?
2. How does work get done cross-functionally?
3. What are the centers of excellence?
4. What areas are lagging?
5. How do the functions work together?
6. How do divisions or business units work together?
7. What role do distributors play building the company strategy?
8. How much discussion occurs cross-functionally?

Processes and Systems

1. What are the organization's core business processes?
2. Are these processes documented?
3. Are they followed?
4. Are there points at which the processes fall apart or get changed by employees?
5. What are the decision-making protocols?
6. What are the standard operating procedures?

Technology

1. How does the organization use technology today?
2. What technology platforms are being used?
3. How does the technology strategy align with the corporate strategy?
4. What knowledge management system is used to share information across the organization?

People and Organization

1. How is the company structured?
2. Are competencies, roles, and responsibilities clearly defined?
3. What is the talent management strategy?
4. Is there a formalized succession planning process?
5. What compensation and reward programs are in place?
6. What learning and development programs are available for employees?
7. How engaged and motivated are the organization's people?
8. How is employee engagement measured?

Leadership

1. How does the company approach leadership development?
2. Who are the current leaders and rising stars?
3. Who are the high-potential employees?
4. What leadership development programs are available?
5. How well does the management team work together?
6. What is the talent succession planning process?
7. How is this plan managed?
8. Are there any leadership issues that will inhibit the business's progress?

Rewards and Recognition

1. How does the company handle rewards and recognition?
2. How does the company provide feedback, and are the feedback systems aligned with the strategy and goals?
3. How are the rewards and recognition systems working?
4. What behaviors do these systems drive?

Communication and Engagement

1. How does the organization communicate?
2. What communication tools are used?
3. Are the communications effective?
4. Are the messages consistent?
5. What do people say about communication and leadership interactions? Too little? Too much? Too formal or informal?
6. What communications support will I have?
7. How do people expect me to communicate?

Culture

1. Describe the organization's culture.
2. How does work get done?
3. What subcultures have been identified, and how would you describe each?
4. How are decisions made?
5. What are the authority protocols?
6. What actions are reinforced or discouraged by leaders, processes, people, and systems?
7. Where is the culture of the organization most prevalent?

Business Results and Outcomes

1. How are results reported?
2. Does the company use specific scorecards, metrics, or data to manage the business?

External Environment

1. Who are the key external stakeholders?
2. What impacts do they have on the organization?
3. Who is important for me to meet in my first three months?
4. How do the external constituents (customers, consumers, shareholders, suppliers, vendors, community, government, regulators, and competitors) affect the company?
5. What are the expectations of board members, customers, markets, and others?
6. What issues should I know about before I start connecting with people?
7. Who can assist me with introductions?

CHAPTER 12

80/20 Zero-Up

● ● ●

*"Simplicity, simplicity, simplicity! I say, let your affairs
be as two or three, and not a hundred or a thousand;
instead of a million count half a dozen, and keep your
accounts on your thumb nail. ...Simplify, simplify. Instead
of three meals a day, if it be necessary eat but one;
instead of a hundred dishes five; and reduce other
things in proportion."*

—HENRY DAVID THOREAU, *Walden; or Life in the Woods* (1854)

WE MET HENRY David Thoreau one chapter back. You probably
wouldn't want him as a customer. In fact, you probably couldn't
get him as a customer because he bought almost nothing from
anybody. He built his famous shack in the woods at Walden Pond
on land his friend Ralph Waldo Emerson let him use for free. As
for building the house, the labor was all his, the materials were
few, and the cost, even in 1840s dollars, was almost negligible.
He kept a careful account:

Boards .... $ 8.03½,
mostly shanty boards.

Refuse shingles for roof sides 4.00

Laths 1.25

Two second-hand windows with glass	2.43
One thousand old brick	4.00
Two casks of lime	2.40
	That was high.
Hair.	0.31
	More than I needed.
Mantle-tree iron	0.15
Nails	3.90
Hinges and screws	0.14
Latch	0.10
Chalk	0.01
Transportation	1.40
	I carried a good part on my back.
In all	$28.12½

So, that takes care of shelter. *Food*? Look at the quotation that starts off this chapter: "Instead of three meals a day, if it be necessary eat but one; instead of a hundred dishes five…" That leaves only clothing to buy. In *Walden*, Thoreau writes

A man who has at length found something to do will not need to get a new suit to do it in; for him the old will do, that has lain dusty in the garret for an indeterminate period. Old shoes will serve a hero longer than they have served his valet,—if a hero ever has a valet,— bare feet are older than shoes, and he can make them do. Only they who go to soirées and legislative halls must have new coats, coats to change as often as the man changes in them. But if my jacket and trousers, my hat and shoes, are fit to worship God in, they will do; will they not? Who ever saw his old clothes,—his old coat, actually worn out, resolved into its primitive elements, so that it was not a deed of charity to bestow it on some poor boy, by him perchance to be bestowed on some poorer still, or shall we say richer, who could do with less? I say, beware of all enterprises that require new clothes, and not rather a new wearer of clothes. If there is not a new man, how can the new clothes be made to fit? If you have any enterprise before you, try it in your old clothes.

No, Henry David Thoreau may not be anybody's idea of a great customer, but he'd make one hell of a CEO, manager, or anyone else whose job was to apply 80/20 with a vengeance.

Thoreau went to live at Walden Pond, he explained, "to front only the essential facts of life." If you think he was taking things to an extreme, well, I admit, he's not for everybody. But consider that much of what he wrote in *Walden* can be distilled into one of his own terse observations: "Our life is frittered away by detail." Who among us has not felt this—and more than a few times? Perhaps you even said these very words, the very words of Henry Thoreau. And perhaps, as a CEO, executive, manager, or business owner, you have found yourself wishing you could start over with a clean sheet of paper or a blank computer screen. Start again without all those unwanted, unproductive details forcing you to fritter away so much of your time.

Perform a Thought Experiment

What if your only customers were the 20 percent who generated 80 percent of your revenue? Imagine that. Imagine that your only customers were your top customers in quadrants 1 and 2.

One of the many breakthroughs credited to Albert Einstein is the *Gedankenexperiment,* literally the "thought experiment." It is a bold technique for projecting the results of a what-if scenario, a future state that does not yet exist and may never exist. It is an exercise of the imagination—subject, however, to certain rules. For a thought experiment is not just a flight of fancy. It is a mental model or logical argument made within the context of a hypothetical scenario—one that may even be contrary to known facts—yet the thought experiment never descends into pure fantasy.

Take your business. Chances are, roughly 20 percent of your customers are responsible for roughly 80 percent of your revenue. I ask that you conduct a thought experiment based on the counterfactual that those 20 percent are your *only* customers. Now, ask, "What would it take to serve *these* customers, who are my *only* customers?" Put it another way. Given the opportunity to size your business appropriately to serve the '80s and only the '80s, how would you make the very most of this enviable situation, using only the best people you currently employ?

To conduct this thought experiment successfully, you need to identify your top performers. This is not quite as straightforward as it might sound. You may have a good idea of the top performers in your current organization, but that organization does not serve only the top 20 percent of its customers. So, while you may know what it takes to serve 100 percent of your customers, you don't really know what it takes to optimally serve the 20 percent who matter most. You must, therefore, exercise your imagination (within the bounds of logic) to define what it takes to be an A player capable of serving A customers for every role required in your organization when it is reduced to serving a customer base 80 percent smaller than its factual counterpart. Apply this A-player definition to your actual pool of resources and match those resources to the requirements of each job. Not every customer will make the cut.

Now Scale Back Up

So far, your thought experiment has been based on scaling down, reducing the business size to serve A customers (20 percent of your actual customer base) and (in your imagination) jettisoning the rest. Now that you have shrunk the company, you need to identify what it would take to acquire more A customers to transform the entire company into a quadrant 1 business. What would it take to focus the sales effort on only A customers?

This is what we call "zeroing-up." It is a reality-based exercise of imagination designed to balance (or rebalance) the business by establishing (or reestablishing) the necessary level of resources to serve the critical few in preference to the trivial many. The objective is to eliminate the *destructively disproportionate* volume of scarce resources required to serve the bottom products and customers, especially in the bottom customer/product quadrant, quadrant 4.

Refocusing your resources requires eliminating underperforming employees and the underperforming customers they serve. You don't do this to punish either set of underperformers but to improve or even save your company. The point to remember is that your underperforming customers are making it difficult, maybe even impossible, to adequately serve your best customers. And if you are underserving your most profitable customers, you will not only lose them, but you will neither create nor attract more of them.

It is, therefore, urgent that you reallocate resources from the bottom to the top to create or attract more A-level customers. These, after all, are your raving fans, and zero-up is the most accurate and efficient way of converting customers into fanatics— not by magic but by selling to them strategically, serving them more effectively, and curating lines of products and services that your A customers clamor for.

The Zero-Up Process

Zeroing-up is the next logical step after focusing and segmenting, but it is a somewhat controversial third step after the 80/20 segment and focus process. It has one goal and one goal only: to help you establish or reestablish the business with the level of resources necessary to serve only the '80s and to serve them optimally. This goal is reached by reducing or eliminating the disproportionate volume of resources it takes to serve the bottom products and customers, especially those of quadrant 4. Now, some managers find zero-up somewhat impractical to apply. For this reason, I have given it its own chapter apart from segmenting and focusing. I do believe, however, that it is an exercise worth running, a way of clearly visualizing the business in a state ideally optimized according to 80/20.

It is a matter of balancing the company, resources, and customers. Lack of balance in a business is not just ugly, it is, in the long run—which may not be all that long—fatal. In business, disproportionality is destructive. The more resources you devote to B customers and B products, the more destructive the disproportion becomes. Not only do you squander effort and assets by overserving unprofitable customers, but you also dilute your ability to serve your high-performing customers adequately, let alone optimally. You will fail to satisfy them, which means you will lose them. What is more, you will be unable to replace them by creating or attracting more of them. Disproportionate allocation of resources is an urgent existential problem for your business. Think in terms of rearranging the deck chairs on the *Titanic*. (Hint: It's a deadly waste of time.)

There is no quick fix for a business incapable of converting B customers into A customers and A customers into stark raving fans. What is needed is focusing energy and resources now and doing so not with the aim of a quick fix but of starting from scratch and doing it right.

Now, the thought experiment that enables you to wish away the trivial many so that you may better serve the critical few, while necessary, will only get you so far. After all, in the real world, you almost certainly cannot afford to scrap everything and start from scratch. What you can do, however, is identify a segment of the business and effectively start from scratch with that segment, building *only* what is needed to support its limited set of customers and products. The goal here is not to allocate costs for the current company but to dedicate only the resources and costs necessary to run the segment you are starting from zero. Zeroing-up this way, segment by segment, reveals the hidden costs of complexity while also surfacing areas where costs can be reduced or removed.

Let me assure you that you are more familiar with zeroing-up than you think. That's because we all do it—or know we should—with our household budgets. Most successful family budgeting begins when you ask, "How much money do I need for the month?" The month about to begin is the segment on which you focus, and you answer your question by starting with zero—that is, starting with a zero base, which is why this budgeting method is called zero-based budgeting.

Start with zero, and then add up the individual costs of what is needed for this month—this segment—only. When you have your total, see how it stacks up against what you are taking in this month. Resolve the difference by either subtracting from your spending (which probably means subtracting some or all your "wants" while leaving in place only your needs) or by adding to your income. Next month, start from zero again, rinse, and repeat.

I don't think anybody is foolish enough to try to create a zero-base budget for the next five or ten years, let alone for their entire projected lifetime. But a month at a time, starting from scratch, is doable—and so is zeroing-up 80/20 for your business. You start from the ground up, building a budget and allocating resources from zero. As you identify the assumptions that drive the business, you add to the wants, needs, and means of attaining them.

Zero-Up Flavors

There is no one right way to zero-up. Use what works best for you. How do you know what works best? Try several ways. Try them all if you must. This is a time to be pragmatic. The *right* approach is the one that *works for you* to yield the optimal view of the business.

The most common methods for zeroing-up are

- By quad
- By market segment
- By product segment
- By product/customer inflection point

Whatever approach you take, you will likely find that significantly more than 80 percent of your profits—typically 150 to 200 percent—are made on the 20 percent of customers/ products that generate 80 percent of your revenue. Vilfredo Pareto was right about the productivity of his pea plants, and he was right about business, including your business.

This 80/20 thing is more than a curious truth. It yanks back the curtain on the vast resources required to support the 80 percent of customers and products that generate just 20 percent of the revenues. So, take a good look. And then realize that it doesn't have to be this way.

Let's consider the two most widely used zero-up methods, quad zero-up and product/customer inflection point zero-up.

Quad Zero-Up

In this approach, you begin with your most recent 80/20 quad chart. The example I show here is typical. Quadrant 1 in this chart represents the 20 percent of customers driving 80 percent of revenue and the products driving 80 percent of revenue, which (in the case of *this* company at *this* time) make up 64 percent of the revenue. This small number of customers and products creates roughly two-thirds of the revenue, a proportion typical of most companies.

The other quadrants here are also typical. Quadrant 2

represents the 20 percent of customers buying 80 percent of the products, making up roughly 16 percent of the revenue. This is the same customer set as in quadrant 1 but includes most of the company's products. Quadrant 3 contains 20 percent of A products but now has 80 percent of the customers (the B customers), representing roughly 16 percent of the revenue. Finally, quadrant 4, the "price up or out" quadrant, contains 80 percent of the customers (B customers) and 80 percent of the products (B products). It represents just 4 percent of the revenue.

Items

A = 875 Products **B = 10,397 Products**

1	**2**
Net Sales = $353,162,402 (64.7%)	Gross sales = $99,069,165 (15.5%)
Material Margin = $236,311,094	Net Sales = $83,335,746 (15.3%)
Material Margin % of Net Sales = 66.9%	Material Margin = $54,042,606
Customers = 93	Material Margin % of Net Sales = 64.8%
Items = 875	Customers = 93
	Items = 9,654
3	**4**
Gross sales = $95,639,992 (14.9%)	Gross sales = $29,109,923 (4.5%)
Net Sales = $83,757,081 (15.3%)	Net Sales = $25,581,984 (4.7%)
Material Margin = $54,884,733	Material Margin = $15,022,407
Material Margin % of Net Sales = 65.6%	Material Margin % of Net Sales =58.7%
Customers = 998	Customers = 988
Items = 93	Items = 9,007

A = 93 Customers / B = 1,005 Customers — Customers

Fig. 12-01: 80/20 Quad example

Getting started with the quad zero-up process is simple. Focus only on the quadrant 1 customers, products, revenues, and material margin. In our example, there are $353 million in net sales, a material margin of $236 million, and just 93 customers and 875 products. Now commence your thought experiment. Build a company and P&L as if quadrant 1 were the *only* business, the *entire* business. Determine the bare minimum of cost needed to support this business: payroll, variable manufacturing overhead, fixed manufacturing overhead, selling, general, and administrative expenses (SG&A), and all other attached costs until operating profit for quadrant 1 (which is the entire thought-experiment company) has been reached.

Remember, this is a thought experiment—a counterfactual act of the imagination that is nevertheless based on reality. So, don't make the error of allocating costs based on your current spending, headcount, and P&L. For the experiment to succeed, the P&L must be constructed from scratch. That's why it's called a zero-up.

When you have built the quadrant 1 P&L—showing how to optimally run just this quadrant (as if it were the whole business)—set it aside for the moment and turn next to quadrant 2 and then quadrant 3. Repeat the quadrant 1 exercise for each of these, building a P&L for each, from scratch, as if each were the whole business, a business you are determined to run optimally. For each of the three quads, keep track of the spend required and the headcount. When finished, your effort will have produced potential optimal future-state P&Ls for each quadrant, along with the headcount needed to support each quadrant and a running total.

Take a step back now and admire what you have done.

You will see that quadrant 1, serving just 20 percent of the customers in your current (real, not imaginary) company, requires substantially fewer resources and headcount to run optimally than the other quads in the business. The total operating income in quadrant 1 is typically 150 to 200 percent of your current profit. Take note of how the leftover headcount compares to the total number of employees.

This is quad zero-up. And if it seems to you that we have forgotten something—quadrant 4—you are quite right. We have forgotten it because, in this thought experiment, we must forget it, as in getting rid of it, unless we can price up the products in this quadrant and move some into quadrant 3.

You are finished with the quad zero-up thought experiment. Congratulations! Of course, you still have a lot more to do because all you have is an experimental image of a potential future state. To put this image into a strategy and, from there, into an executable business plan, you and your organization must do the hard work of development and execution.

Product/Customer Inflection Point Zero-Up

The most basic view of 80/20 is simply a set of top-down lists with the highest revenue-producing customer/product at the top and the lowest at the bottom. Typically, this view demonstrates that a large fraction of a company's customer base and product offerings generate inadequate revenue. This is in line with the 80/20 principle, of course. Nevertheless, aside from affirming the principle's validity, the list has limited practical use in zeroing-up. In business, *revenue* is not what finally counts. *Profits* are the measure of success.

We need to determine which customers are profitable and which are not. We want to serve the profitable customers and serve them so well that they become our raving fans. We want to retain them and figure out how to convert as many of our B customers into A customers as possible. To do this, we perform an inflection point zero-up analysis. In this case, the "inflection point" is a line that separates profitable from unprofitable customers.

Here is the thought experiment that will help you draw this line. Imagine you lead a brand-spanking new company. Until you fully imagine it, it isn't real. Or, rather, it is a zero—without a plant, employees, products, customers, or any assets. So, start the experiment. Grab your top-down customer list. Take from it your best customer and move that customer to the pristine new company. That done, calculate the absolute bare minimum cost required to support this customer. Factor in material costs, variable payroll, variable manufacturing overhead, fixed manufacturing overhead, SG&A expenses), and other attached costs until you reach the earnings before interest, taxes, depreciation, and amortization (EBITDA) *for that one best customer.*

Now, move down to the next customer, the number two on your top-down list. Repeat the exercise. When you finish with customer 2, repeat the process to the bottom of your list. You will end up with EBITDA for each customer and a running total. You will discover—eureka!—that as customers are added during your descent down the list, the running-total EBITDA for this pristine new company increases at a decreasing rate. Plot this cumulative EBITDA graphically, and you will have a (probably lumpy) bell curve. It rises, fluctuates here and there, and then begins to flatten out. At some point, after you add the next lowest customer in line, the curve will inflect frankly downward. In other words, at this point, *adding* the customer *lowers* your company's overall EBITDA. Generally (though often with some exceptions), adding each customer after the inflection point is reached further lowers overall EBITDA.

As I just pointed out, there are some exceptions. You may find some customers on the lower end of your list that contribute positively to EBITDA, and you may also find some customers higher up on the revenue scale who violate the general rule that the more productive the customer is in terms of revenue, the more profitable. Reorder your customers by their EBITDA so you have a true bell curve without hills and valleys. Now, locate the peak of *this* bell curve. Everything to the right of the inflection point represents customers that eat away at your company's profitability.

As with the quad zero-up method, completing the product/ customer inflection point zero-up thought experiment is not in itself sufficient to guide change for your company, but it is a starting point for the development and execution phase of the 80/20 process. Remember, too, that a curve is a curve and not reality in all its granular splendor. The inflection point need not dictate simply dropping customers and products. Alternative strategies, such as those in the "Dirty Dozen," are available. As with the application of all process models, thinking is required. That said, zero-up based on locating inflection points can be applied to customers, products, and employees in a quest for strategies to create maximum efficiency.

CHAPTER 13

Lean

"There's never time to do it right, but always time to do it over."

—JOHN MESKIMEN, *Wall Street Journal,* March 14, 1974

THE BRITISH AMERICAN philosopher Alfred North Whitehead (1861-1947) started his academic career as a mathematician. In chapter 5 of his 1911 *An Introduction to Mathematics*, he wrote, "Civilization advances by extending the number of important operations which we can perform without thinking about them." I believe this remarkable statement was why he moved from mathematics to philosophy, in which field he is best known for having invented "process philosophy."

Why should you and I care about this?

First, anyone, regardless of profession, who says that the advancement of civilization depends on the ability to perform important operations without thinking about them has the makings of a great business leader. Second, process philosophy quietly overturned a few thousand years of received wisdom and made possible, among much else, high-efficiency, high-performing business—business driven by "lean thinking."

Since the time of the heaviest hitters in the history of philosophy, namely Plato and Aristotle, most people have viewed the world as a collection of things, of enduring substances. In this view, processes are regarded as transient and less worthy of our attention than "things" in all their permanence. The Socratic philosopher Parmenides declared change a kind of illusion, and Aristotle himself thought that change was accidental. In process philosophy, Whitehead argued that changes—processes—are the only true elements in the everyday real world that we all share. Whatever we are and whatever we do, it is all about process.

Lean

Lean is a widely used methodology for improving the performance of a business. If Professor Whitehead were still among us, he would applaud lean as process philosophy in action. He would see it as an advance in civilization by extending "the number of important operations which we can perform without thinking about them."

Of course, what Whitehead should have added to his formulation was that getting to the point where "we can perform [operations] without thinking about them" requires a great deal of thinking. The best way to drive the necessary thought process is by asking and answering five key questions:

1. What does the situation require?
2. What is the problem we are trying to solve?
3. What is the near-term target condition?
4. What is the long-term goal for the business?
5. What is important to customers?

Thoughtfully answering these questions will go a long way toward *not* doing something stupid, like throwing a million bucks at a nickel problem. Lean is best viewed through 80/20 glasses. The 80/20 approach will tell you what is worth aiming at and what is not worth the price of an arrow. Once you have decided to aim, lean can tell you a lot about how to hit the target. Armed with the answers to the five questions, the organization can begin its "lean transformation." The following must be examined, analyzed, and opened up to change:

1. Human resources
2. Leadership and management systems
3. Basic mindset

All must be evaluated with the goal of lifting the business from good to better. Experience has shown that at least three actions are critical to the success of any lean transformation. They are the introduction of—

1. ***Standardized work***, which is the meticulous application of demonstrated best practices. In short, the best ways to perform "important operations... without thinking about them."
2. ***Visual management***, by which operations, especially manufacturing operations, are reductively translated into visual scoreboards, charts, and Gannt charts by which teams can see, readily evaluate, and improve their own performance.
3. ***A plan, do, check, act framework*** in which improvements can be structured on a team level.

Lean Manufacturing and Lean Thinking

The historical predecessors to lean can be found in the concept and methodology of *scientific management* as formulated at the end of the nineteenth century and beginning of the twentieth by Fredrick Winslow Taylor, who studied all manner of manufacturing and production processes to dramatically increase both their quality and efficiency. Taylor was indeed the father of "standardized work," with the standard founded on close observation and measurement.

Few discussions of lean, however, even give Taylor a perfunctory nod. Instead, they start with the evolution of the much-celebrated "Japanese miracle," that country's remarkably swift and successful economic and industrial recovery after its devastating defeat in World War II. Moreover, these discussions typically focus specifically on the operational models the Toyota automobile company introduced and soon dubbed "the Toyota Way." More formally, this was called the Toyota Production System (TPS). It was developed in 1948 and continued through 1975 as a response to postwar Japan's general scarcity of finance and resources. In such an environment, the chief enemy was identified as *waste* (in Japanese, *muda*), which came in seven varieties known (for obvious reasons) as The Seven Wastes:

1. Waste of overproduction (the largest waste)
2. Waste of time on hand (idly waiting, the second largest waste)
3. Waste of transportation (inefficient production space)
4. Waste of overprocessing (bureaucracy, red tape, redundancies)
5. Waste of excess inventory
6. Waste of movement (as on the shop floor)
7. Waste of defects (fixing, redoing, discarding)

Having defined the enemy, Toyota knew clearly what to do: defeat the enemy—kill *muda* in all its forms. TPS attacked *muda* by designing ways to eliminate "overburden" (*muri*) and "inconsistency" (*mura*) in all manufacturing processes. The two best-known weapons against *muda* and the causes of *muda* (*muri* and *mura*) were *just-in-time* and *Jidoka*. JIT is the principle of making only what is needed, only when it is needed, and only in the amount or quantity needed. *Jidoka* is a Japanese word signifying a special type of automation, a hybrid of completely mechanical and automation with a significant human element or "human touch."

Driven by postwar necessity, the Toyota Way was the first practical incarnation of what came to be called lean manufacturing. Years later, lean manufacturing was extended into "lean thinking." The phrase was coined in 1988 by John Krafcik, an MIT mechanical engineer best known for his work on Google's autonomous driving (driverless vehicles) technology unit.

In 1985, MIT had formed an International Motor Vehicle Program to study the new Japanese manufacturing techniques. MIT went well beyond manufacturing proper. In addition to applying lean thinking to factory operations, supply chain coordination, engineering, and product design, the MIT program applied lean to market assessment, sales, and service. In each dimension of the added scope, however, the enemy remained *muda*, waste, specifically the waste that is the unintended consequence of how a process is organized or poorly organized. Lean thinking sought to minimize waste by organizing all processes, both inside and outside the factory, according to five principles:

1. Value
2. Value streams
3. Flow
4. Pull
5. Perfection

Lean thinking aims to create in a business a *lean culture*, which creates and sustains growth through aligning customer satisfaction with employee satisfaction. The products and services of a company operating within a lean culture are necessarily innovative. Their profitability must be achieved without unnecessary costs to customers, vendors—and, significantly, to the environment.

In a lean culture, every employee is trained to identify wasted time and effort in their job and to work together with others to improve processes by eliminating waste. Thus, people are given primacy in a lean culture. It is *people first*, employees as well as customers. If everyone in the organization buys into the culture—and shares the same essential mindset, values, and assumptions—the company will be enabled to deliver greater value at lower cost and price while simultaneously developing in each worker the confidence, competence, self-efficacy, and ability to work with others.

How Lean Thinking Applies the Toyota Way

MIT's International Motor Vehicle Program closely studied how the Toyota Way enabled the automaker's remarkable journey from bankruptcy in the early postwar years to dominance in the industry by the 1970s. The first important MIT insight was that the company relied on a combination of master teachers—*sensei*—and coordinators or trainers. These people focused on helping Toyota managers think about processes in a lean way and from, first and foremost, the perspective of their jobs.

They began with the *workplace* itself. Upper-level managers were asked to go to the shop floor and observe, close-up and in real time, work processes and conditions. The value of walking around the shop floor is multilayered. First, it shows managers what is going on. Second, it shows workers—the shirtsleeves people creating tangible value—that their leaders care about and respect them. Third, it allows managers to ask questions of the workers, and fourth, it allows those workers to speak directly to their bosses and share their ideas and insights. This opens up the possibility of giving employees a platform for independence and initiative in creating or adding to processes and best practices.

Having gathered information from the shop floor, the managers can begin to do the hard work of applying the five principles to the current situation in their plant.

1. **Value:** Leaders must define value through their customers' eyes and accept that value is conveyed to customers through built-in quality. This implies that customer satisfaction, paramount in value creation, must be built in at every step of every process. Product features must create satisfaction. Quality must create satisfaction and be built into every production step. As for flow in the manufacturing process, the principle of built-in quality dictates that production be halted at every doubtful point so that defective work can be caught and corrected before it proceeds down the line and, God forbid, into the marketplace.

2. **Value streams:** Products must be visualized as the embodiment of value. The company creates value streams, which must flow continuously and on pace. "Takt," or "Takt time," is the product assembly duration required to match the flow rate with the demand rate. Takt can be determined by calculating the ratio of open production time to averaged customer demand. Achieving an accurate takt means the company will produce neither too much nor too little concerning demand. This synchronization of production with demand is essential to just-in-time manufacturing. It avoids the waste of overproduction and the lost sales of underproduction. Achieving takt requires stable teams working on a standardized set of products with standardized equipment in a standardized way.

3. **Flow:** To ensure that value flows to the customer, businesses must abandon the traditional production

approach of thinking in terms of batches, which dictates that once work is set up in one way, it is important to make as many pieces as possible to maintain lower unit costs. Lean thinking looks at this differently. It seeks to optimize the flow of work to satisfy real demand *now*, not some projected (that is, imaginary) demand next month. Aligning current flow with current demand should come close to achieving "single-piece flow" rather than batched flow. This dimension of JIT substantially reduces the cost of business by minimizing or even eliminating the need for warehouses, and it reduces the volume of transportation costs for shipping.

4. **Pull:** Calculating takt (principle #2) helps the company change from the traditional approach of *pushing* products (value) and instead letting the customer *pull* products (value). In this way, production flows at the rate the customer needs. This alignment of production with pull is aided by *kanban*, cards (physical or digital) that are used to track production within a factory or line. Their use is valuable in synchronizing production (push) with demand (pull). At its most basic, work items are represented by kanban cards. Process steps are represented by vertical lanes (usually labeled *to do*, *doing*, and *done*) on a graphical representation called a kanban board. The board represents an individual, team, or organizational process from beginning to end. The lanes on the cards move left to right from one lane to another—from *to do* to *do* to *done*. The leftmost lane effectively represents the backlog. This is where new requests (pulls) are put before they are prioritized by the individual, team, or organization.

Unlike serial status reports, the kanban cards and kanban

board allow managers—and everyone else involved—to see all at once where everything is. Ideally, workers update the boards themselves. Everyone is involved. Everyone is accountable to everyone else. Pull and push are more easily coordinated, and problems appear in real time on the board. It is pull that generates healthy creative tension in the workplace. The guiding idea is that each action in the process should be incited by a request—a pull—so that waste is minimal. Pull is essential to lean.

We come now to the final lean principle, #5—*perfection*. In lean, *kaizen* (continuous improvement) is applied in the quest for perfection. In contrast to traditional notions of inspection of work and strict supervision of each process, kaizen takes a lesson from the ancient teachers, the sensei. The sensei did not so much teach facts as they sought to develop the kaizen spirit in every student. In a lean shop, the quest for perfection is inculcated as a commitment on the part of each worker to incrementally improve processes by working together step by step. Kaizen seeks one hundred 1 percent improvements from everyone every day, everywhere, rather than a single 100 percent leap forward by a maverick worker. Incremental improvement as a commitment embeds lean thinking in the mind of each worker. This is what, in time, creates a lean transformation.

Any lean transformation can be summed up in this equation:
$$Job = Work + Kaizen$$

Scaling Kaizen

In practice, kaizen can be scaled in several ways.

Point Kaizen

Point kaizen is spontaneous and happens in real time. When a product, assembly, component, or process is defective, immediate actions are taken to correct the problem before the work item proceeds.

System Kaizen

System kaizen is an action on a larger scale. It is not spontaneous but planned and organized to address systemic issues in an organization. It is a method of strategic planning to be applied over a brief duration to produce a system-wide effect.

Line Kaizen

When improvements are communicated upstream or down within a process, you have a line kaizen. Communication can flow in either or both directions.

Plane Kaizen

In this kaizen, several lines are connected (forming a "plane") such that an improvement in one line is implemented in others as well.

Cube Kaizen

Cube kaizen extends line and plane kaizens throughout the organization and even to suppliers and customers.

Scope and Impact of Lean

In 1990, the results of MIT's work on Toyota's process innovations became the basis of a book by James P. Womack, Daniel T. Jones, and Daniel Roos, *The Machine That Changed the World*, which was followed in 1996 by Womack and Jones's *Lean Thinking*. These volumes are basic to a full appreciation of lean thinking, but the bottom line speaks compellingly. Compared to the rest of the automotive industry, TPS used

- ½ the human effort in the factory
- ½ the manufacturing space
- ½ the investment tools
- ½ the engineering hours

- ½ the time to develop new products
- And produced a 2x level of quality

Applying Lean

Lean, of course, is useless until it is applied. Get beyond description and theory to application by adopting a kaizen mindset to achieve three overarching goals:

1. Reduce waste
2. Improve quality
3. Improve safety

These goals are met not in a single leap but through kaizen, continuous incremental improvement.

Apply lean thinking to management using approaches focused on cost-cutting while enhancing the value stream. The objective is to continuously develop employees and improve processes to create value and prosperity using the least possible resources. Lean approaches should, therefore, solve real business problems and improve how work is performed at each level of the company and in each activity. The improvements should be made continuously and in real time and aim to address root causes.

While processes are both the focus and vehicle of applied lean thinking, people create and execute every process. For this reason, lean thinking always puts people first, and the company must provide people with the skills to solve real business problems and improve how their work is performed.

By definition, kaizen consists of continuous incremental improvement, but do not lose sight of the big picture. Improvement is about taking the whole organization from its existing state toward an improved state. This journey is a continuous and relentless small-step progression, within a lean transformation framework, from purpose to process improvement to people development.

Purpose

Take a situational approach to framing each lean transformation by asking at the start, "What—specifically—does this situation require?" Answer the question in the context of purpose by defining the objective of the transformation and, specifically, what business problem you expect the transformation to solve. Answering these big questions always requires answering more tightly focused questions relating to the details of the situation at hand, such as

- Do we need to improve at the workstation, department, value stream, company, or cross-company level?
- What is our long-term goal for the business?
- What is the problem we are trying to solve?
- What is the near-term target condition?
- What is important to our customers?
- What are our underlying assumptions and mindset?

Process Improvement

For process improvements on the team level, apply basic problem-solving tools and skills to your understanding of the seven wastes. Use kaizen to devise incremental improvements. For larger process and system-level improvements, focus on how the work and associated information flows by eliminating *muda*, *muri*, and *mura*. Define the existing situation (present state) and frame the improved situation (future state).

People Development

Bear in mind the model of the sensei. Traditional Japanese sensei did not so much teach facts as they sought to develop the kaizen spirit in each of their students. Thus, we should strive to create in each employee a spirit—a mindset—of continuous improvement through kaizen events. These range from quasi-spontaneous team efforts to address a specific problem to more formal workshops with set goals for improvement in a specific area.

- A specific problem is identified.
- The time in which the problem occurred or is occurring is specified.
- The area or part of the operation affected is defined.
- The problem is described.
- The degree (severity) of the problem is described.
- Who is being affected by the problem is established.
- The impact of the problem is assessed.
- The cost of the problem is quantified.

Depending on the scope of the issue, a brainstorming session may be sufficient to arrive at a solution, or a more extended event/workshop must be set up to include data collection, idea generation, and implementation.

Not all human resources developments are centered on kaizen events. Training, especially on-the-job training (OJT), is used, hands-on projects may be employed, and formal training is necessary.

70-20-10

At the time lean was becoming widely adopted, a new approach to training was emerging. It is based on the 70-20-10 model for learning and development. The foundational principle of 70-20-10 is that workers at all levels derive 70 percent of their knowledge on the job, that is, from job-related experiences. An additional 20 percent comes from casual interactions with others, and—stunningly—just 10 percent of knowledge is derived from formal educational events.

The model emerged in the 1980s; the product of research on what makes a manager successful was conducted by Morgan McCall, Michael M. Lombardo, and Robert A. Eichinger of the Center for Creative Leadership in Greensboro, North Carolina. Many organizations have found the 70-20-10 model valuable in guiding the structure of their training programs.

Hands-on experience (70 percent in the formula) is the most effective training because it enables employees to discover and refine their job-related skills. It improves decisions and gives practical experience in overcoming challenges and productively interacting with bosses and mentors. Especially valuable is the opportunity to make mistakes and learn from them in a constructive environment that delivers immediate feedback on their performance.

An additional 20 percent of knowledge comes from social learning, coaching, mentoring, collaborative learning, and general peer interaction. The components of encouragement and feedback are the major benefits of the social approach. Only 10 percent of professional development is derived from traditional coursework and formal educational events.

70-20-10 is a good argument for OJT, provided that the OJT environment is supportively structured and does *not* rely on a wasteful and potentially dangerous sink-or-swim approach.

Elements of Applied Lean Management

It is helpful to think of lean management in terms of five basic elements: standardized work, visual management, team-level improvement, project-based improvement, and policy deployment.

Standardized Work

"Civilization advances by extending the number of important operations which we can perform without thinking about them." Thus spake Alfred North Whitehead. Standardized work applies to specific operations and captures the best method currently known by which each operation can be performed. Employees are trained in this method for each operation they perform. The standards are institutionalized throughout the organization.

Standardized work aims to attain optimal performance in all operations performed, whether in the office or on the shop floor. For the company, standardized work is the best practice and, as such, is relied on by everyone. Because standardized work is stable, it is far more capable of supporting continuous improvement, which, by definition, is lean leadership behavior.

True kaizen can exist only in an environment of standardized work. When improvement depends on occasional and random big improvements, the improvement is rarely enduring, let alone permanent. Big improvements tend to become smaller with time. For this reason, it is better to have one hundred 1 percent improvements over time than a single 100 percent one-time improvement. The small incremental improvements in the context of standardized work create large, cumulative, enduring improvements.

Visual Management

As mentioned earlier in the chapter, visual management enables everyone on a team, department, or even an entire company to see the current situation in context and at a glance. This simultaneous and instantaneous view greatly impacts the serial, selective, and delayed delivery of formal status reports conveyed narratively. In short, work systems using visual management— kanban, posted charts, simple timelines, progress graphics, color-coded Gannt charts, heat maps, and the like—enable *anyone* to go into *any work situation* and distinguish normal from abnormal *right now*.

Visual management is simple but high impact. It can promote a close to real-time response to deviations from target conditions. For this reason, it is embedded into every aspect of lean, at the process, system, and strategy level. The visual approach surfaces opportunities for kaizen.

Team-Level Improvement

Team-level improvement is instrumental in engaging the entire organization in continuous improvement. Structured team-level improvement aligns each team's improvement efforts with the business's strategic objectives. Although the incremental improvement is focused by the team on the team, it is managed through so-called *glass wall* management. This is a term for open communication throughout the organization, including sharing information with everyone and inviting everyone to participate in and contribute to each team's incremental improvement. Walls still exist, but their transparency counters the traditional tendency toward the creation of silos, which leads to suboptimization throughout an organization.

Transparent team-level improvement spills over into the entire company, improving problem-solving and kaizen skills across the organization. In the aggregate, team-level improvement creates an auditable process by which the organization's engagement in continuous improvement can be monitored and improved.

Project-Based Improvement Using PDCA

Project-based improvement applies the continuous incremental improvement approach to the output of teams and their projects. The basic tool for this improvement program is PDCA—plan, do, check, act—a straightforward sequence for affecting improvement and, ultimately, the lean transformation.

> **Plan:** Begin by establishing objectives and the processes required to achieve them.
> **Do:** Deliver the objectives, collect data, and note results.
> **Check:** Based on the data and results from the *do* stage, evaluate the results. The data must be compared to the anticipated outcomes from the *plan* phase. Note all similarities and differences between expected and actual outcomes. Evaluate any test procedures used. Look for any changes from the original test created during the plan phase. The data from the first three phases should be plotted on a chart (in other words, use *visual management*) to make it easy to see trends as the PDCA cycle is repeated multiple times. This will aid in deciding which changes work, which work better than others, and which don't work at all.
> **Act:** The *act* phase is where a process is improved, so some prefer to call it the "adjust phase."

Records created from the do and check phases identify problems with the process, such as nonconformities, opportunities for improvement, inefficiencies, and any other issues that produce less-than-optimal outcomes. Based on these records—which are most effectively presented visually—the team seeks the root causes of problems, investigates them, and devises ways to eliminate them. At this stage, risk is also re-evaluated.

The expected outcome of the act phase is a process improved with better instructions, standards, and/or goals. Moreover, a fully evaluated PDCA run will provide the baseline for planning the next PDCA cycle. The subsequent cycle's chief improvement objective is to avoid repeating the problems identified in the previous cycle. If the error repetition does occur, the team has still made progress, having learned that the action taken was ineffective and more PDCA iterations are therefore required. This is not failure but incremental progress through knowledge gained. When a newspaper reporter asked Thomas Edison for a progress update on his incandescent electric light development—a promised innovation closely followed by the press and public— the inventor replied that his progress was slow. He had tested some ten thousand potential materials and processes to create a viable filament for the lamp. None of them were satisfactory. The reporter asked him if this "failure" discouraged him. Edison famously replied, "I have not failed. I've just found ten thousand ways that won't work." Fortunately, working out most problems requires fewer than 10,000 PDCA cycles, but persistence is nevertheless required.

Policy Deployment

The phrase "policy deployment" is frequently used in US management to describe a strategic planning process that emphasizes creating synergy and synchronization among corporate goals, management planning, and daily operations. Lean management often uses a Japanese figurative translation of policy deployment, *hoshin kanri*. We can break down *hoshin* into its constituent syllables, *ho* and *shin,* meaning "direction" (*ho*) and "needle" (*shin*). Put these together, and you have the Japanese word for "compass." Like *hoshin, kanri* can be broken down into its constituents—*kan* means "control" and "*ri*" means "logic." This may be rendered in English as "management control." It is much easier to understand the meaning of "policy deployment" as it is used in lean management if substituted with the Japanese terms. Put another way, in lean, policy deployment is the process that identifies and aligns all resources in the business to accomplish a set of major improvement initiatives to give the company a competitive advantage.

Executed successfully, *hoshin kanri* will achieve the company's strategic objectives with the least possible resources— the ideal both 80/20 and lean aspire to. *Hoshin kanri* must work successfully in both the short term, on the level of each team's day-to-day functioning (that is, it must work "*in* the business"), and in the long term, in the overall transformation of strategic objectives to achieved strategic initiatives (it must work "*on* the business"). The process is summarized in the chart that follows.

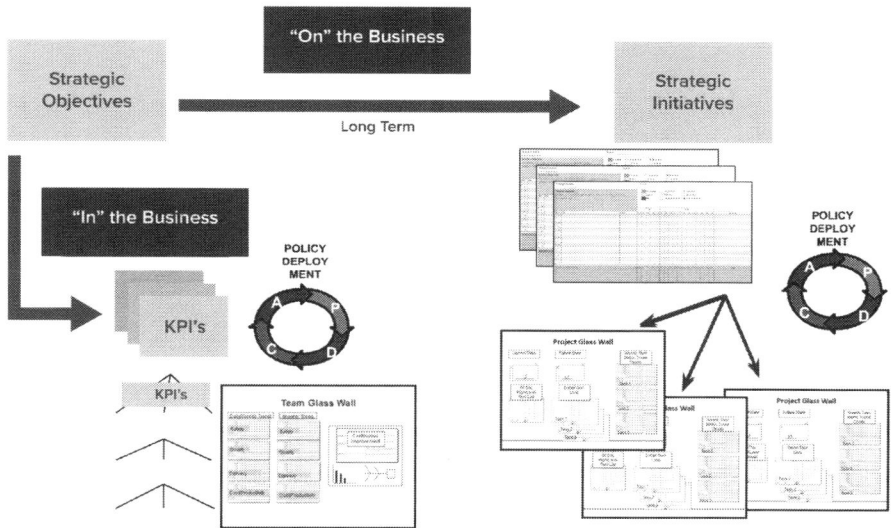

Fig. 13-01: Lean Management applied to policy deployment

This chart encapsulates the dual perspective of lean management applied to policy deployment. It is a check/reflect process carried out through repeated iterations of PDCA cycles, which are subjected to periodic kaizen events or other reviews to verify progress toward successfully executing strategic objectives and for making corrections and adjustments as necessary. The frequency of the reviews depends on the nature and scope of the initiative involved. For many projects, weekly reviews are appropriate, but the interval may also range from daily or weekly to quarterly. Successful outcomes from the review, PDCA, and kaizen process include not only the achievement of targeted results but the acquisition of a deeper understanding of the business and, within each employee, a strengthening of critical thinking skills and the development of a kaizen mindset.

CHAPTER 14

Talent

* * *

*"Surround yourself with the highest caliber people.
Remember that first rate people hire first rate people—
while second rate people hire third rate people."*

—RICHARD M. WHITE, JR., *The Entrepreneur's Manual*

CREATING A SUCCESSFUL growth strategy for the business requires attracting diverse sources of talent, continually assessing and developing the organization's bench, aligning people with the needs and objectives of the business, rewarding employees for performance in a competitive and motivating way, and engaging every employee in the pursuit of the company's strategy and vision. These are the elemental components of strategic hiring and talent development.

Hiring Is a Strategic Matter

At the top of this chapter, I quoted a guy named Richard M. White, Jr. I don't know anything about him, except that back in 1977, he published a book called *The Entrepreneur's Manual*. I confess I haven't read the book, but this quotation from it, which I stumbled across, offers a sharp insight: hire the best people you can get, not just because they can probably do the job well but also because they will tend to perpetuate excellence by hiring the best people when it becomes their turn to do the hiring. Settle for second best, and you will begin the company's decline because people whose performance is subpar will almost certainly (when it is their turn to hire) tap people they are confident will not outshine their dim light. In short, excellence begets excellence. Anything short of excellence initiates decline.

But there's a catch to this simple formulation. Robert Half (half of the Bob and Maxine Half who founded what is today Robert Half International Inc., a big brand-name international human resources consulting firm) wrote in *Robert Half on Hiring* that the "best person you interview isn't necessarily the best person for the job."

Now, terms like "first-rate" and "best" are very useful *in a general way*. But strategic thinking is not about making critical decisions *in a general way*. Critical decisions always involve qualifying general principles or value statements in terms of the strategic imperatives of *your* business in the context of *present* needs and a vision for the *future* as embodied in the business plan.

For example, the "best person you interview" may demand more compensation than you can afford "for the job" at hand. Perhaps he or she is overqualified. Do you really need Albert Einstein to fill a slot in accounting? (Well, probably not. But take note of two things: 1. Before he was recognized as a genius, Einstein made his living as a patent clerk in the Swiss patent office. From all reports, he enjoyed the work and was very good at it. 2. He famously quipped, "The hardest thing in the world to understand is income tax." So, resist the temptation to pigeonhole people.)

Perhaps the most common hiring error is failing to think strategically and instead yielding to a reflexive impulse to automatically favor those who exhibit what can be described as the trait of dominance. Those with this trait or behavioral style want immediate results, have a bias for action, accept challenges, and make quick decisions. They are problem solvers who also question the status quo. In short, to almost any manager who interviews them, they come across as leaders. What could be wrong with that?

Nothing—provided that the strategic imperative of the job in question requires a leader. An NFL team fields just eleven players at any one time, only one of whom is a quarterback. A team that puts eleven quarterbacks on the field is doomed. No team manager, scout, or owner would ever hire quarterbacks exclusively. The game's strategic imperatives demand various traits, talents, and behavioral qualities or styles to attain the goal of victory.

Hiring is a strategic matter. It is not simply a case of securing the "best" person, but the best person for the job. Jobs usually come with specific requirements, including experience, training, education, applicable certifications, and so on. Equally important, from a strategic point of view, is assembling a team that brings together the right people with the right behavioral styles in the right positions. DiSC is a very familiar tool many HR professionals use to identify four major behavioral styles in job candidates. We have already mentioned the *D* behavior—dominance—usually associated with leadership. There is also *I*—influence. Influencers excel at contacting people, verbalizing, generating enthusiasm, entertaining people, and participating in a group. They tend to be infectious optimists. In the right positions at the right time and place, influencers are indispensable.

In DiSC, *S* stands for supportiveness. People who prominently exhibit this behavioral style generally perform consistently and predictably. They exhibit patience, are driven to help others, show loyalty, and are good listeners. *S* individuals are invaluable when it comes to creating a stable and harmonious work environment. The final style DiSC recognizes is *C* for conscientiousness. People who manifest this style pay close attention to standards and key directives. They concentrate on important details, meticulously weigh any decision's pros and cons, and strive for and check accuracy. They are systematic workers who analyze performance critically.

Recruiting and developing human resources in an enterprise is a strategic task that seeks to align subject matter expertise, experience, and behavioral style with an array of key roles that contribute to the success of the company and serve to optimize performance.

The Top Talent Values

Five values should be in recruiting and developing talent:

1. **Talent is a strategic matter.** This one is at the heart of HR in the service of strategy. Talent and the talent mix are intrinsic parts of any high-performing business. Talent must be aligned with every business process, policy, and objective.

2. **Diversity is an asset.** We live in a diverse world, and our workforce should reflect this. Today, more than ever, the ability to attract and retain diverse talent creates a competitive advantage.

3. **Development is aligned with the requirements of the business.** Learning and skills development should focus on the specific skills and competencies the company needs to perform at its best today and with an eye toward future development and growth.

4. **Employee engagement is a key value.** As the nineteenth-century American sage Ralph Waldo Emerson wrote, "Nothing great was ever achieved without enthusiasm." Aligning and motivating teams to create passionate business performance will drive continuous improvement in the context of profitable growth.

5. **Developing and nurturing talent is everyone's business.** A talent mindset must be embedded in the organization and pursued relentlessly.

Driving Talent Imperatives

Recruiting and developing talent is valueless as a *theory* or an *aspiration*. It must be a central *activity* of the business. This requires, first and foremost, defining the organization's talent needs in specific terms. To satisfy these needs, initiatives must be developed to—

1. **Attract** diverse sources of talent.
2. **Assess and develop** the required talents in individuals, teams, and the company as a whole.
3. **Align** people with the business needs and objectives, putting the right people in the right places at the right times.
4. **Reward** people for performance in ways that are both competitive and motivating.
5. **Engage** everyone throughout the enterprise to pursue the company's strategy and vision.

The Talent Management Process

A standardized talent management process must provide tools and procedures for supporting each phase of the talent cycle.

Attract

There are five phases in the process of attracting new talent:

1. **Define the need.** Start by identifying, describing, and justifying the needed role. Enumerate the essential duties, skills, and competencies required. Create an ideal candidate profile. You will also want to specify the

reporting relationship, the market compensation for the job, and any deviations from the going market rate that may be deemed desirable or necessary.

2. **Source the talent.** Identify appropriate sources, favoring a diverse pool. Filter for the right qualifications. As appropriate, consider both internal and external applicants, including outsourcing.

3. **Select.** Screen qualified candidates through résumés, interviews, assessments, and reference checks. Look beyond education and technical qualifications to also consider behavioral style. Think about the candidate's potential place on the team and desirable contributions.

4. **Offer.** Formulate an offer that includes the full terms of employment: base pay, short-term and long-term bonuses, healthcare and retirement benefits, and such additional benefits as a company car, relocation package, and so on.

5. **Onboarding.** When the candidate becomes an employee, follow a prescribed process for onboarding, including integration of the new employee into the company and its culture. Onboarding must address any relevant financial, ethical, legal, and safety instructions and create a familiarity with the tools, people, and information the newcomer needs to become productive.

The target outcome of the talent acquisition process is complete alignment between the business need for the role, the role specification, the qualifications of the candidate selected, the market rate of pay (or justification for deviation from it), and a complete onboarding plan and process.

As a process, talent acquisition can be successfully modeled on other standard processes in the company. It needs a clear-cut objective: finding, attracting, hiring, and onboarding top talent to meet identified business needs. The process itself should be systematic and repeatable. The process should be standardized across the entire enterprise to the degree possible.

Attracting talent to your business should attempt to emulate best practices for the most effective recruiting and hiring methods. Continuous improvement may be applied to the process to ratchet up the quality of candidates hired. Recruiting and hiring work best in an environment where each new hire can quickly begin to positively impact the organization.

The tools and content of talent attraction and recruiting include

1. A detailed job description, with an emphasis on the key responsibilities and essential requirements (level of experience, training, education, and so on).

2. Looking first to current employees as your best go-to option; post the new position internally for three days before launching external recruitment.

3. Performing a compensation analysis to determine competitive pay for the role (but be prepared to justify deviating from market rates if there is a compelling reason to do so).

4. Securing an appropriate recruiting contract if you use an external recruiter.

5. Requiring a résumé and/or curriculum vitae (CV) from each applicant.

6. Creating a candidate application form soliciting information most useful to strategic hiring.

7. Securing the candidate's authorization to obtain information verification.

8. Reviewing all references received and discussing them with the candidate during the face-to-face interview.

9. Ensuring that the employment offer extended to any

candidate is fully and properly authorized, including all required signoffs.

10. Issuing a comprehensive employment offer letter as well as supporting information such as healthcare details, bonus plans, and relocation package.

11. Enclosing any employment agreement (if one is used) with the offer letter.

Assess and Develop Talent

Talent assessment and development begin soon after a new employee is onboarded, but these processes are formalized in an annual employee review. The object of these annual reviews is to evaluate capabilities and competencies, identify behavioral styles, and create personal development plans. Think of these processes as *development management*, which, like all aspects of strategic growth management, has continuous improvement as its chief objective.

For each employee, the assessment and development process includes

- Aligning with the employee on a set of performance objectives and ensuring the employee understands his or her role in the context of the company strategy
- Identifying areas for improvement as well as growth in career development
- Putting into place plans for further development and growth through training, job rotation, project work, and on-the-job training
- Providing ongoing constructive feedback and coaching
- Assessing actual performance results versus potential; this provides the basis for annual merit and bonus recommendations

The assessment and development process aims to assure and improve alignment with the overall strategy, create clarity and accountability, promote continuous performance improvement, and sustain passionate engagement. The process is interactive, requiring commitment on the part of management and the employee.

Achieve Clarity

While personal, friendly, spontaneous, responsive, and ongoing coaching is indispensable to fostering continuous improvement, managing development and growth requires standardized documentation. Employees deserve a measure of explicit clarity and objectivity in the evaluations they receive. Documentation also serves to avoid misunderstandings that can lead to anything from poor performance to dismissal to litigation. Developing standardized forms for annual performance reviews and individual development plans is best. The review form should include, at a minimum, expectations and key deliverables for the upcoming year, what metrics will be used to assess performance, required competencies to be achieved, the key ratings, and three to four personal development initiatives to be completed within the next year.

Enable Progress and Achievement

Words like "improvement" and "growth" are inherently vague. To make progress and achievement possible, make progress tangible by setting clear expectations, checking in and providing feedback throughout the year, and assessing performance at a year-end review.

1. **Setting Expectations.** The manager and employee should meet at the start of the year to set and agree upon

performance expectations for that year. In addition, together, they should identify development activities to be completed. This first phase should occur within the first six weeks of the new year (fiscal or calendar year, as applicable).

2. **Check-In and Feedback.** Two to three times during the year, the manager and the employee should meet to review progress toward achieving expectations. The objective of this check-in and feedback is not merely measurement but improvement. So, expectations and objectives may need to be reviewed and modified, especially if conditions or priorities have changed. All changes must be agreed to and documented.

3. **Assessment.** At the end of the year (calendar or fiscal, as applicable) but before merit and bonus recommendations are submitted, the manager and associate should again meet to review the year's performance and results produced. At this time, assessment of performance, attainment of core competencies, and identification of improvements required and opportunities to be leveraged are made. Objectives for the coming year are also discussed.

Desired Positive Outcomes of the Assessment and Development Process

The assessment and development process can be considered a success, year to year, if the employee experiences—

1. Increased motivation to perform
2. Increased self-confidence
3. Understanding of clearly defined roles, expectations, and strategic alignment
4. Realization of development opportunities

For the manager, a successful outcome is characterized by—

1. A fuller understanding of the team member's capabilities and level of performance
2. Increased productivity and improved results
3. Avoidance of major problems, thanks to timely and ongoing discussion and feedback

The company also wins if the development process produces—

1. Improved communication of the strategy, goals, and the individual employee's strategic role
2. Alignment of efforts toward the strategic goals
3. Stronger connection with and support for a pay-for-performance culture
4. Identification of high-potential employees for future opportunities
5. Insight into training and development needs across the company

Align

By the end of 1944, World War II in Europe looked to be all over but the shouting. The Allies were in a celebratory mood. (General Eisenhower called it "victory fever.") Then, on December 16, in the Ardennes, a thickly forested region in Belgium and Luxembourg, a huge Nazi armored force suddenly broke through Allied lines. It was a stunning development.

How did it happen? Without question, the combined Allied forces far outnumbered and outgunned Hitler's badly depleted army. It turns out that even the best-equipped, best-trained, and most committed people in the world will be useless if they are not available in the right place and ready at the right time.

On December 16, 1944, the Ardennes was inadequately defended by a relatively small number of American soldiers, a combination of battle-weary units sent to rest and recuperate in what was deemed to be a "quiet sector" and some as-yet untested units, mostly green National Guard troops.

Because the Americans here were outgunned and outnumbered, the enemy made a rapid breakthrough. US high command scrambled to get massive reinforcements to the Ardennes, especially to the town of Bastogne, where the US 101st Airborne was surrounded. Fortunately, the most capable field commander the Allies had in Europe, General George S. Patton Jr., was confident that he could rapidly march his Third Army to the scene. That force had been advancing on the southern end of the war's western front and was now some ninety miles south of the Ardennes. Turning 350,000 troops ninety degrees to the north after they had been engaged in continuous combat for three months—and doing this during the worst weather in the coldest winter in modern European history—was a very tall order indeed. But Patton was keenly aware that transforming defeat into victory depended on having the right people in the right place and time. The Third Army made the turn, made the march, and broke the back of the last German war offensive, turning a costly and demoralizing Allied setback into a massive victory.

It was called the Battle of the Bulge, and it can serve as a lesson in talent alignment, the multistep process that ensures you have the right talent in the right place and time.

Chances are that you don't have a General Patton on staff. So, it is important to ensure you will not be caught short or have to move heaven and earth to instantly find the people you need. To avoid this situation, it is necessary to put into place a talent-alignment process—*now*:

1. Identify the company's immediate and future talent needs regarding the capabilities required to successfully execute the strategy and the specific subject-area knowledge, experiences, and competencies for critical roles. Evaluate

current readiness and what will be required for the longer term. If necessary, work on the company's organizational structure to ensure it best supports its strategy.

2. Inventory the talent currently available in the company. Analyze it in terms of key strengths, skills, and capabilities. Identify individual employees with high potential—candidates for leadership roles and ambitious assignments. Identify current pipelines to ensure adequate bench strength. This includes identifying potential successors for critical management roles—individuals who are ready now or can be made ready quickly.

3. Identify talent gaps that leave the company exposed. Build action plans to close those gaps by hiring (acquiring new employees), renting (taking on consultants or temporary workers), and developing available internal talent.

4. Check talent status regularly, including through formal leadership talent review sessions.

A successful talent-alignment process facilitates an accurate assessment of talent needs and available talent. The desired alignment will always further the company's growth strategy and should be integral to the 80/20 management process. You will need to define the current and future organizational structure that will optimally support strategy execution. Critical to defining this structure is first articulating the key roles and readiness of available talent to fill them. Define the traits, behavioral styles, technical skills, leadership skills, and experience needed for each critical role. Based on the emerging picture, evaluate available talent and the gaps that need to be filled.

Through appropriate sequencing and timing, optimal alignment delivers the "ready now" talent to support the company's strategy. The process should be carried out proactively to prevent losing competitive advantages.

Reward

People are motivated by many things, but never underestimate the universal power of cash rewards. *Base pay* must be competitive in the marketplace and appropriate to job responsibilities. In addition, *benefits* (such as health, income protection, savings, and retirement programs) can be valuable in terms of motivation, performance, and retention. As with base pay, benefits need to be structured in the context of marketplace competition. Some positions and circumstances call for *perquisites (a.k.a. perks)*, such incidental benefits as using a company car in jobs requiring significant travel.

Bonus and incentives are variable compensation over and above base pay, benefits, and perquisites. These should be formally pegged to performance measures and metrics clearly stated in company policy. It can be useful to divide these into short-term incentive compensation (STIC) and long-term incentive compensation (LTIC). STIC bonuses are typically based on annual performance metrics. This bonus comes in the form of a cash award. LTIC bonuses are based on longer-term (such as three years) performance measures. They are intended to motivate employees to think and act in the best long-term interest of the company to continuously enhance the company's value. LTIC bonuses may be cash awards, stock or stock options, which give the employee an ownership stake in the company and are highly appropriate for focusing on the long term.

However leadership structures compensation, certain objectives should figure in any sound compensation plan:

- Compensation should be fair and appear fair—clear and transparent.
- Compensation should be competitive to both attract and retain superior talent.
- Compensation should be accompanied by clearly

expressed accountabilities.

- Compensation should reward performance, motivating employees to go the extra mile to achieve superior results.
- Compensation should reinforce ethical behavior in all practices.
- Compensation should scrupulously align the interests of management with those of shareholders.
- The compensation structure should maintain a significant portion of "at-risk compensation" for senior leaders with greater responsibility.

Fairness, competitiveness, and transparency within a merit-promoting culture of pay-for-performance are the hallmarks of an effective reward system. Under no circumstances should the reward structure ever appear personal, arbitrary, random, inconsistent, or capricious. Leverage pay-for-performance by standardizing all bonus evaluations based on performance, results, contributions, and potential assessments.

CHAPTER 15

M&A

"The big-business mergers... have all the appearance of dinosaurs mating."

—JOHN NAISBITT, *Megatrends* (1982)

MOST BUSINESS HOW-TO books lay out strategic growth strictly in terms of organic growth, which proceeds from the company's internal resources. M&A? It may be mentioned and even considered, but it's not something you can teach in a book. Or maybe it's regarded as something you should not teach in a book because it is somehow not part of the core skill and process set executives need. There is an unspoken sense that companies that grow organically are more authentic than those that engage extensively in mergers and acquisitions growth strategies.

This is a prejudice, and I don't like prejudice. You might say that I'm prejudiced against prejudice. But I need to confess that, one way or another, all the preceding chapters have addressed strategic growth pretty much exclusively as organic growth. This chapter makes amends for that. It lays out a set of workable processes for successful growth through M&A, believing that inorganic growth can, should, and perhaps even must play a vital role in strategy execution.

That said, a single caveat at the outset is in order.

John Naisbitt was a futurist with a CV pedigree that included a stint as an assistant to JFK's commissioner of education and proceeded on an upward trajectory through think tanks and consultancies (including his own) as well as a Harvard fellowship and professorships at Moscow State University, Nanjing University, and Nankai University. His first book, *Megatrends: Ten New Directions in Transforming Our Lives*, was published in 1982 in fifty-seven countries, sold some fourteen million copies, and largely monopolized the number one slot on the *New York Times* best-seller list for two solid years. He died in 2021 at the enviable age of ninety-two, long enough to have seen some of the future he predicted and probably some he failed to predict.

Now, I mention all this because each of the ten megatrends he defined in some way included the assumption that people and businesses would become increasingly decentralized, with hierarchies replaced by networking and institutional help via self-help. He compared the near-mania for M&A in the 1970s and 1980s (when he researched and developed his book) to "dinosaurs mating." In other words, M&A was an activity primitive, clumsy, and doomed to extinction.

About many mergers and acquisitions, this was and still is spot on. When carried out impulsively, non-strategically, desperately, or as a substitute for (rather than strategic addition or alternative to) organic growth, the process and outcome tend to be primitive and clumsy. Heed Naisbitt's warning, but don't accept his observation without qualification. Like any other mode of business growth, M&A requires integration with the company strategy and execution via a rational process.

This chapter details M&A in eight critical dimensions:

1. Acquisition strategy development
2. Sourcing of deals
3. Evaluation

4. Due diligence
5. Negotiation
6. Documenting and closing
7. Integration
8. Transaction measurement

Acquisition Strategy

Going to the supermarket without a thoughtfully drawn-up shopping list is the surest way to waste time and money. The same goes for M&A. First and foremost, any mergers and acquisitions must make sense within your overall 80/20 business strategy. The purpose of an acquisition strategy is to apply a clear logic for identifying M&A targets that will create value within the framework of the company strategy.

This does not rule out opportunistic M&A. But truly value-creating opportunities outside of the company strategy are rare indeed.

In addition to serving the company strategy, your M&A strategy must provide a rational understanding of transaction size and frequency: the types of transactions that suit the strategy, including add-ons, adjacencies, and entirely new platforms, and what attractive acquisition candidates look like in terms of their attributes and characteristics.

Acquisition Process

As with every strategic business function, acquisition benefits from a clearly established process.

1. While there are many ways to measure earnings, I use EBITDA, not just because it is a comprehensive measure but because it is the key valuation metric used in my field, private equity, which generally lasers in on finances. Begin with a firm understanding of the long-term (usually

three- or five-year) goal from the perspectives of revenue and EBITDA. For example, I led a company with a five-year goal of $2.6 billion in revenue and EBITDA of $550 million.

2. Next, determine your "go-get," which, in its simplest form, is the gap between your goals and the strategic forecast.

3. The go-get will determine the size of acquisitions to pursue to fill the identified gap.

4. With these basic measurements now on the table, determine the attributes of attractive acquisition candidates. Consider, at minimum, these four dimensions:

   A. **End markets:** Are you comfortable with the sector in which the acquisition target operates and the geographic and end markets it serves? In answering this, consider the anticipated growth trends of the underlying markets, the demand for the target's products or services, competitive industry dynamics, and the target's historical and projected cyclicality.

   B. **Strategic and cultural fit:** You propose bringing someone new into your family. Think hard about how this target company will make for a strong strategic and cultural fit with your existing portfolio and how it will align with your corporate strategy.

   C. **Operational characteristics:** Look for the characteristics you believe will enhance shareholder value.

   D. **Financial attributes:** Don't neglect the primary financial attributes. Most desirable are strong revenue and earnings growth potential, solid operating profit margins, and a high cash return on investment (CRI). CRI is the consolidated cash flow from operations minus mandatory expenditures plus customer prepayments, the sum of which is divided by gross investment, plant and equipment, plus primary working capital (inventory + AP-AR). In short, CRI = cashflow/(primary working capital + gross property, plant, and equipment).

In addition to these general measures of attractiveness, you want to be very specific about identifying and including acquisition criteria in your process. Create clarity on precisely how any acquisition candidate will serve to facilitate the operating company's strategic goals. Is it filling a product gap? Is it claiming new territory? Define the applicable *strategic* goals and measure the candidate against these.

Timing

M&A should follow the completion of your annual SMP so that top management can prioritize sourcing in terms of transaction size, frequency, and types of transactions that the corporate development team should develop.

Sourcing

Sourcing is developing channels for potential deals and then leveraging those channels to identify specific acquisition candidates. Sourcing is necessary to develop and manage a reliable and consistent pipeline of potential targets that meet your acquisition criteria.

The sourcing process calls for establishing and maintaining a strong external network. You will need to develop relationships with investment banks, private equity funds, and others to create deal flow. The leadership must work closely with its constituent operating companies to identify opportunities for M&A that will contribute to their meeting strategic goals. In addition, management should leverage key sources of information from outside the company. Engage with consulting firms as appropriate in search of potential deal flow opportunities, and work with financial advisers to conduct external searches of companies that align with your strategic goals.

At the level of operating companies, managers should continually identify opportunities by leveraging their business knowledge and relationships with key customers, suppliers, and competitors. These opportunities should be brought to the attention of the internal deal team, which should use its customer relationship (CRM) capabilities to evaluate the opportunities and, as appropriate, add them to a database of targets.

Sourcing is a continuous task. In the end, however, it has but one goal: building and maintaining a robust and attractive deal pipeline. Sourcing can achieve just three acceptable outcomes with respect to this pipeline. It can

1. Create an active pipeline of actionable, attractive acquisition targets
2. Create a non-active pipeline of attractive acquisition targets that are *not* currently actionable
3. Remove non-attractive targets from the active pipeline

Evaluation

When sourcing delivers a viable M&A prospect or prospects, the evaluation process begins. This comes before due diligence and is a prerequisite to due diligence. A top management function, often called a corporate development group or investment committee, seeks input from other appropriate sources, such as an operating company or a division, and assesses the target as an investment opportunity. At this stage, the analysis should determine whether the target has sufficient potential to warrant spending significantly more time, resources, and money on evaluating it through a formal due diligence process.

Essentially, an acquisition has two types of deal flow: an auction or a proprietary deal. Each requires a different evaluation process.

Process for Evaluating an Auction Flow

In an auction flow, there is usually a teaser, often a concise PowerPoint presentation, which summarizes the potential sales process but (to maintain confidentiality) without naming the target company. Nevertheless, you should expect the teaser to include such information as

- Industry overview, describing the industry and the competitive landscape in which the company operates.
- The business, including the company's capabilities and type of products or services offered.
- Location, identifying the company's headquarters and various sites. This is important from the perspective of strategic geographical alignment.
- Financial summary, offering the potential target's financial profile and including forecasts of EBITDA margins and other relevant financial metrics.
- Investment rationale, value-based reason(s) to buy the business, such as recurring revenue, enterprise customers, concentrated customer base, proprietary platforms, patents held or controlled, etc.
- Customer overview, highlighting key customers that build or bolster the company's credibility.
- Transaction structure, laying out the nature of the transaction as expected by the seller: complete sale of the business, a carve-out, venture financing, and so on.

- Bankers' information, which details whether the sale process is taken up by an exclusive banker or is a joint venture by two or more banks. This section furnishes banker contact details.

Use the teaser information to assess the attractiveness of the opportunity. If the opportunity appears attractive, execute a nondisclosure agreement (NDA) and obtain and review the confidential information memorandum, then evaluate the strategic fit of this acquisition by affirming alignment with the company strategy. If alignment is confirmed, conduct preliminary due diligence and initiate a full analysis, including market research (as applicable).

- Perform a preliminary valuation analysis, from which deal memos, a target profile, a scorecard, and any other necessary materials are prepared.
- At this point, the opportunity can be vetted with the company's investment committee or equivalent body.
- Assuming the deal passes muster with the investment committee, draft and submit to the target company an indication of interest (IOI). If invited, attend any management presentation and update the valuation model based on any new information.
- Acting on the latest information, once again review the opportunity with the investment committee or its equivalent.
- If the investment committee approves, submit an updated letter of intent and present the target's response to the banker, M&A committee, or its equivalent.

Process for Evaluating a Proprietary Deal Flow

A proprietary deal flow differs from an auction flow in that a specific buyer—your company—can acquire the target company before that company is presented to others. Proprietary deals are typically presented to a buyer based on a perceived fit between the target and the prospective buyer. From the perspective of a seller, a proprietary deal has the advantage (usually) of closing faster than an auction.

The obvious first step is for the prospective buyer to evaluate strategic fit through company research. Before engaging with the seller, an NDA should be executed. If initial research tends to confirm that the company represents a good strategic fit, a conference call with the target's management and/or owners is in order to obtain a fuller understanding.

If the target remains attractive after these preliminary steps, obtain from the target financial statements, both historical and projected, and carry out a preliminary valuation analysis. If the light is green, prepare deal memos, a profile of the target company, and other essential information to forward to the investment committee or its equivalent for their vetting.

Based on the response of the investment committee, a nonbinding IOI should be drafted and submitted to the target company. The response is then presented to the M&A committee with all updates.

Outcomes

For all the complexities and nuances of the acquisitions process, at this point, whether the deal is an auction or proprietary, only two outcomes are possible: the target company remains attractive because it aligns with the buying company's strategy, and the process, therefore, advances to due diligence, or the target does not align with the buying company's strategy, and that company withdraws from the process.

Due Diligence

President Ronald Reagan is credited with the motto "Trust but verify." He borrowed it from the Russians, for whom it has long been a familiar proverb, and he used it in the context of Cold War-era nuclear disarmament. His message to the Russians and Americans was that we could trust the Soviet Union as long as we verified everything their officials reported or promised.

"Trust but verify" is the perfect meme for a key stage of any acquisition. After you have a full picture of the target company, including all their claims, financial statements, and other relevant documents, it is time to verify and deepen your understanding of the target. Due diligence looks for potential financial, legal, and regulatory exposures while enhancing your understanding of the company's structure, operations, culture, human resources, supplier and customer relationships, competitive positioning, and outlook. Now, you should have a pretty vivid picture of these things at this stage. What you are looking for now is focused less on opportunities than on pitfalls, yellow lights, and red lights. Something found in due diligence may well prompt you to kill the deal. Assuming the M&A process has been efficiently pursued up to this point, it often turns up aspects of the proposed deal that require some modification. At the very least, due diligence will help to ensure that this still-prospective acquisition represents the best decision at the right time and for the right cost.

And, by the way, it is helpful to think of due diligence as bidirectional. That is, you are putting the microscope on your target, but you should also be reflecting on what issues or problems, if any, need to be addressed when integrating the acquisition into your company. That roadster would look nice on your driveway, but is it worth acquiring when what you really need is a minivan to haul the kids?

While due diligence involves some hard work that typically requires accounting and legal expertise and (potentially) consultation with engineers, marketers, and the like, its purpose is ultimately very simple. Confirm the seller's claims, financials, contracts, customers, and all other pertinent information, and reevaluate your assumptions. The object is to ensure that everyone in your organization is sufficiently satisfied to bring the deal to a close.

Due Diligence as a Process

Due diligence is not subject to any single prescribed process and depends on the nature of both the buying and selling companies. Is the target public? Private? What is the nature of the deal—an acquisition of assets or stock? What is the nature of the markets involved? And so on.

If the buying company has a dedicated corporate development function, it is this team that should lead the due diligence process, coordinating as necessary with appropriate managers in tax, legal, HR, IT, and finance. If a third-party due diligence adviser has been engaged, the corporate development team should oversee these consultants. The due diligence team is typically responsible for five deliverables:

1. Using input from others, including consultants, developing a valuation mode incorporating all due diligence findings.
2. Consulting with legal and finance to identify key issues and set optimal terms for the transaction.
3. Reporting as appropriate to the M&A committee and soliciting the committee's feedback.
4. Preparing communications for the board.
5. Reviewing the purchase agreement.

If applicable, operating companies should assist with the due diligence process, especially in preparation for the post-closing integration planning. Finance must lead in developing an acquisition financing strategy, assessing tax impacts, and proposing structural alternatives to minimize adverse tax impacts. Finance must also play a role in furnishing assumptions for the valuation model. Legal must work closely with finance and corporate development to ensure optimal deal terms.

Due diligence logically follows the evaluation, but the evaluation is tested against due diligence. Indeed, aspects of due diligence should be performed on an as-needed basis. The timing of the due diligence process is quite variable, depending on the nature and complexity of the deal. The typical range stretches from thirty days to six months.

Due Diligence Outcomes

A successful M&A due diligence either confirms or contradicts the initial valuation of the target company, furnishing a complete and accurate picture of the risks and opportunities while also providing information helpful in facilitating the effective integration of the target company into the business.

Specific outcome items include:

1. **A comprehensive understanding of what the company is buying.** A valuation should not be considered valid until it is subjected to due diligence findings.

2. **Necessary detective work.** Like a forensic audit, due diligence requires a detective's mindset, an experienced detective's knowledge, and street smarts. If you do not have such detectives on your due diligence team, hire outside consultants to help.

3. **Find reasons to amend or kill the deal.** Trust but verify. Don't assume the worst, but don't assume the best, either. Approach due diligence with optimistic

skepticism. Look for problems. Look for reasons to walk away. Look for aspects of the deal to modify in structure, terms, or price.

4. **Resist the impulse to fall in love.** Following from point 3, don't let yourself fall in love with this or any deal. Stay frosty. Be prepared to walk away.

5. **Follow the money, but don't be dazzled by it.** Financials are numbers on a page. What you are buying are the people who put those numbers there. General Patton often pointed out that *the soldier is the army*. The alpha and omega of any company are its people.

6. **Perform due diligence as the first phase of integration.** Never forget that you are investigating an entity that will be part of your organization. Use due diligence to gather insights that will accelerate and optimize integration planning.

The Negotiation Process

Everything in this chapter has led to this point: the negotiation. When you acquire a company, you start negotiating only after you have acquired full knowledge of the company; however, aspects of the negotiation take place more or less in tandem with the due diligence process. These aspects include negotiating the purchase agreement itself, the price, escrow requirements, etc. The buyer's objective in the negotiation is *not* to beat up the seller. The objective has nothing to do with the seller. It is all about the money—obtaining good terms and a good price.

As with due diligence, there is no single cut-and-dry sequence for negotiation. That said, the overall process generally looks something like this:

1. The draft purchase agreement is obtained from the seller.
2. The document is reviewed by in-house legal counsel, the

head of corporate development, and possibly relevant outside advisers. In these readings, items are marked for discussion or negotiation.

3. The marked-up draft is returned to the seller for comment. The document may pass back and forth more than a few times as issues are negotiated.

4. Some marked-up items are discussed and presented to the due diligence team for their input.

5. Other due diligence items and issues are incorporated into the purchase agreement draft as they are noted.

Documentation and Closing

After negotiation, a legally binding contract is drawn up and signed. There are two primary ways to purchase a company: a stock purchase agreement or an asset deal. These require extended discussion, which we will save for another book. However the purchase is consummated, the signature marks the closing of the deal, although in the post-documentation period, financial adjustments often need to be made.

Integration Process

Although the deal has been legally consummated, the M&A process is not concluded. Integration, for which planning has already begun, is now commenced in earnest. Plans and a list of key actions are drawn up to optimally integrate the acquired business into the buyer's operations. The integration step is widely viewed as one of the most important phases of the acquisition process.

Unsurprisingly, there is no single, set process for integration, but the key steps include:

1. **Developing a workforce integration plan.** The buying company has just taken on a number—perhaps a

large number—of new employees who must be onboarded and otherwise integrated into the company.

2. **Conduct one more HR due diligence.** Integration is accelerated by the compilation of a human resources profile of the acquired company.

3. **Compare benefits packages.** Benefits need to be harmonized between the acquired company and the buyer company.

4. **Compare compensation.** Differences here need to be resolved in ways that are deemed fair.

5. **Based on points 3 and 4, an assigned integration team is tasked with developing a benefits and compensation strategy to harmoniously integrate the workforce.** The two systems must be fully integrated.

6. **Leadership assignments are made.** The integration team determines leadership needs of the newly structured company, evaluates candidates for leadership, and assigns them.

7. **Duplicate functions must be resolved.** Both acquisitions and mergers typically produce "redundancies." Leadership needs to identify the duplications and either place a duplicated employee in a new position or release him/her from employment.

8. **Clear, centralized, authoritative communication must be established.** Information is extraordinarily valuable. Fail to communicate systematically, and the information vacuum will be filled by rumor, which, beyond anyone's control, benefits no one.

9. **You need measurable data.** Therefore, define transition data requirements. These are the metrics that the integration teams will use to measure the overall success of the integration and guide progress along the way.

What to Do with the Data

Waste no time in beginning to evaluate the acquisition or merger. Transaction measurement should be considered the final stage of M&A. Management is accountable for the results of the M&A. Analysis of early data will determine if the acquisition is meeting, exceeding, or trailing expectations. If early results are disappointing, determine and implement corrective actions. Keep refreshing the measurement used to evaluate the valuation model. Generally, transaction measurement spans the first five years following the acquisition.

How to Avoid an Identity Crisis

For some companies, there comes a time to change their basic identity. Western Union started in 1851 in the telegraph business and was so good at it that the very name *Western Union* became synonymous with American telegraphy from the 1860s through the early 1980s. People stopped saying, "I need to send a telegram," and instead said, "I need to send a Western Union."

What a success story! And what could possibly go wrong?

Telegrams, as a technology, became not merely obsolete but irrelevant—that's what went wrong. But Western Union did not die. Instead, it radically changed its identity from *the* name associated with the telegram to *the* name associated with wire transfers, money orders, money transfers, and bill payments. It was no longer in the electric information transfer business. It was in the electronic money transfer business. And that was a good thing for Western Union.

Such a sweeping identity change is probably not good for your business. Unless the nature of your industry and technology has so radically changed that there is no longer a profitable place for what you do, you need to be very wary about mergers and acquisitions that depart radically from your existing core business.

Profiting from the core is often cited as a timeless strategic precept. Most enduring businesses build their market power on a well-defined core business. This becomes who they are, and that identity confers a significant competitive advantage. There are extraordinary circumstances in which a business needs a radical change, but more often, M&A that takes the business away from its core is not so much a strategic diversification as it is a counter-strategic dilution. It is almost invariably a mistake to diversify in ways that distance your enterprise from its core competencies. Look at the range of potential M&As through this lens.

And, while you're at it, remember to grab one additional lens and a hearing aid.

Examine every dimension of each prospective acquisition through the lens of 80/20. Each addition to the company should serve, protect, and enhance the vital few without adding to the burden that is the trivial many. That vital 20 percent is the core of your profitability.

And the hearing aid?

If you cannot hear the voice of the customer as you contemplate a particular acquisition, stop in your tracks until you *can* hear it. Be certain that you have identified and understand the core needs of customers—your A customers, that 20 percent who deliver 80 percent of your business—before you risk your existing products, channels, branding, and pricing by acquiring a new business. Turn up the volume on the voice of your current best customers.

The bottom line on M&A? *Go buy companies that do the things you're already great at.*

CHAPTER 16

Managing Risk

"A danger foreseen is half avoided."

—THOMAS FULLER, *Gnomologia*, 1732

RISK IS INHERENT in everything we do. It is part of life and, therefore, a part of business. Leaders of organizations, therefore, must manage risk simply to stay in business. But all risk management is not created equal. There is traditional risk management, and there is the proactive and more comprehensive approach known as enterprise risk management (ERM). An approach essential to the strategic management process, ERM is planned and implemented as an integral aspect of, rather than an adjunct to, the business strategy.

Traditional Risk Management
Since ERM is a variant of what we might call traditional risk management, we should begin by looking at that.

Executives manage risk every day, but traditionally, they do this by delegating to business unit leaders the risk management within their areas of responsibility. For example, in the traditional approach, it is not the CEO who manages IT-related risks but the chief technology officer. Cashflow-related risks? The CEO hands these off to the CFO or, perhaps, the treasurer. Sales and marketing risk management may be assigned to a CMO or a sales director or some combination of the two. On and on down the line, each functional leader manages risk on their turf and does so with considerable autonomy.

The chief advantage of this traditional approach is that the risks inherent in a specific function are managed exclusively by the authority and expert. If this seems like good old common sense, well, it is old and common, but recall how Einstein defined common sense: "a deposit of prejudices." The disadvantages of traditional risk management are, in fact, numerous. To begin with, it reinforces existing organizational silos or even creates new ones. Silos within an enterprise promote suboptimization—inefficiency and ineffectiveness caused by focusing on optimizing an individual business unit rather than optimizing the results produced by that unit in the context of the entire enterprise. This may mean that very significant risks looming on the horizon go undetected. Some risks fall between the silos and thus remain unrecognized until the risk is realized in a crisis or a catastrophic event. It is also the case that the same risk may affect multiple silos in different ways. The CMO may recognize a potential risk but might have no idea how it could impact other enterprise functions. Similarly, using the traditional risk-management approach, the head of a siloed operation might respond to a recognized risk in ways that adversely impact other aspects of the business. A frequently encountered example of this is the CIO, who authorizes more stringent IT security protocols without considering the impact on the portals through which customers purchase products.

Even at the CEO level, which deals with the whole enterprise, risk is too often looked at through an internal lens. The C-suite may focus on internal operations, the "business" within the organization's walls, giving short shrift to risks that emerge from outside the business. Lose sight of competitors, especially in a market that is moved by technological innovation, and you will likely miss even obvious competitive threats. The C-suite may also fail to adequately connect risk management to creating the strategic framework and, ultimately, the strategy and the business plan. Bottom line? The traditional view does not fully integrate risk management into strategic planning.

ERM Is Risk Management Integrated into the Strategy

By definition, an effective business strategy encompasses the entire enterprise, as does the business plan that embodies such a strategy. Integrated into the strategy, ERM must, therefore, embrace the entire enterprise in a holistic, portfolio-wide view of risks that threaten the achievement of the priority objectives of the business. ERM takes a top-down view of all the significant risks that may impede the objectives of the business.

Consider ERM a *strategic* leadership process. The risk insights it provides should be cycled into the organization's strategic plan. The more aware of and knowledgeable about potential risks on the horizon, the more effectively the C-suite and board can build strategies sufficiently resilient to avoid or withstand the entire range of relevant risks. The time to consider risk is not when a particular risk becomes a present reality but when the strategy is being built. Such proactive risk planning is not merely a necessary evil (though it is that) but a way to capture and retain competitive advantage by reducing the chances that risks will derail strategic initiatives. And while there is no avoiding every risk, incorporating risk management into the strategy will almost certainly enable executives and managers to be better prepared if a risk materializes and makes an impact.

ERM is a Process, Not a Project

Risks exist and evolve. For this reason, ERM is an ongoing process rather than a single project with a discrete beginning, middle, and end. It is applied throughout PGOS. When the business plan is executed, a feedback loop is created that goes back to the situation assessment that originated in the first hundred days. We can break down this feedback loop in more detail. In the feedback journey, ERM must continuously identify additional emerging or evolving risks, assess their potential or actual impact, design and implement a response, communicate and monitor that response, and modify strategy and objectives accordingly.

We can further detail the ERM process this way:

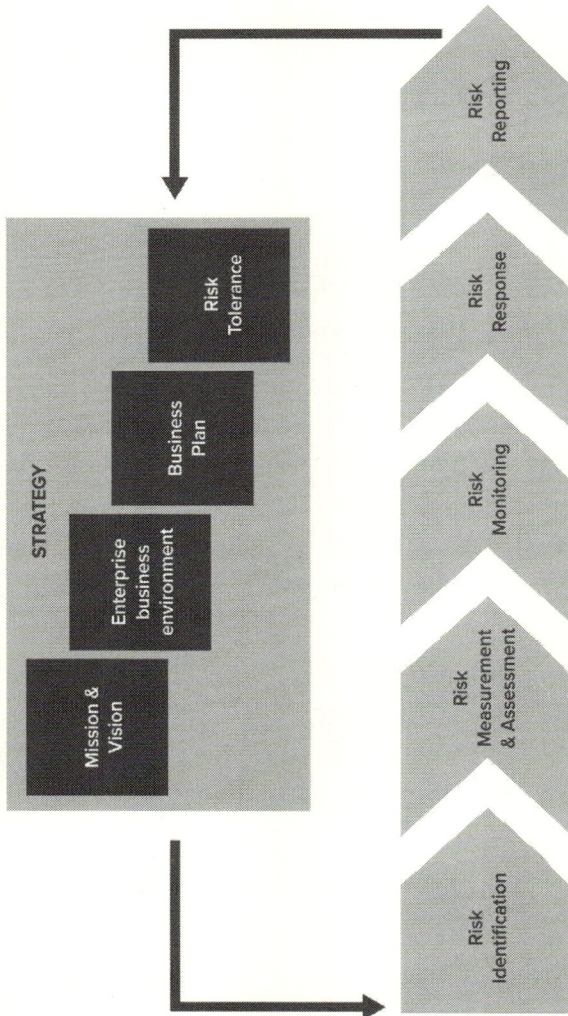

Fig. 16-01: Validation/Reassessment of strategic risk management

As pictured here, the strategy encompasses not only the mission and vision and the business plan but also the business environment of the whole enterprise and a strategic determination of the organization's position on risk tolerance. Each of these four elements of the strategy are formulated and assessed in terms of risk management through six discrete steps:

1. **Creation of a risk register.** Also called a risk log or risk inventory, this is a tool the business uses to document and track risks across the organization. A risk register is typically a spreadsheet with fields relevant to every significant potential or recognized risk. In the creation of a business plan, some of the risks listed will be documented events actually encountered; others will be predicted risks. As the business plan is deployed, some predicted risks will recede in importance while other unanticipated risks will emerge. Thus, a risk register is always a work in progress.

   Various risk register models, templates, and forms are available online. Just bear in mind that all effective risk registers record the information gathered about each threat. Such information includes the nature of the risk, its potential level of impact, the prevention and mitigation measures in place, and so on. A risk register should tell you everything you need to know about every risk predicted or identified.

   Like everything else in business, one size does not fit all. Nevertheless, every risk register should include:

   • **Risk identification**. This is a label, which may be a name or even an identification number. The identification should also note the date of the inclusion of the risk.

   • **Risk description**. A concise description of the risk provides a high-level overview of it.

- **Risk category**. Classify each risk: budgetary risk, external risk, security risk, compliance risk, and so on. This helps to assess the origin of the risk and what members of the organization should be most useful in mitigating it.
- **Risk probability**. How likely is the occurrence of the risk? Decide on standard verbal ratings, such as "not likely," "likely," or "very likely," or create a numerical scale, which might be expressed as a calculated percentage to determine the likelihood of occurrence.
- **Risk analysis**. Gauge the potential impact. Again, choose between standard verbal ratings or quantitative measurements.
- **Risk mitigation (risk response plan)**. As a step-by-step solution to mitigate or eliminate the risk in question, this should include a description of the intended outcome of the plan.
- **Risk priority**. The key to risk management is prioritizing each identified risk.
- **Risk owner**. Who is responsible for monitoring and mitigating a particular risk or set of risks? The "who" may be an individual or a team.
- **Risk status**. The current status of the risk: "open," "in progress," or "closed."

2. **Risk identification distribution.** The risk register should be distributed to those directly involved in risk management. In many cases, this will be a designated risk management committee. During strategy building, the risk register determines the company's risk appetite *for each risk*, both for the short term and the longer term. This is important in building the business plan.

3. **Risk measurement and assessment.** The risk register should be reviewed in an annual meeting, and

the major risks should be (re)assessed to adjust the strategy and/or operating processes, if necessary.

4. **Risk monitoring.** The risk register should be reviewed at set intervals for new risks and changes in the status of existing risks. Again, this current information may impact the operational level or the strategy itself.

5. **Risk response.** The owner/owners of each risk listed on the register are responsible for developing plans for elimination or mitigation. Proposed responses are described in the risk register.

6. **Risk reporting.** A risk report should be prepared for leadership, including the board of directors. At this level, the report should consist of a high-level summary of trends organized by the main risk categories. The corporate strategy team should write and submit the report each quarter. Often, a heat map is used to communicate the relative priority rankings of the top ten risks based on severity and likelihood.

The Enterprise Perspective on Risk

ERM takes risks that ultimately affect the entire enterprise, focusing on those risks that threaten achieving the business's core objectives. This implies that understanding the risks requires understanding all that drives value for the enterprise as defined in the strategy. If—as is so often the case with publicly traded companies—the enterprise prioritizes its anchor products as its crown jewels, the chief drivers of value, then ERM needs to spotlight and deal with threats posed to these products and their markets, including competition and demographic changes. If the company prioritizes growth through new products, a new set of risks comes into play. If the envisioned growth is mainly through acquisition, yet another complex set of risks must be considered.

ERM is proactive, which gives it a bias for the longer term but never excludes short-term risks. For example, a company that develops many new products or services is necessarily oriented to the long term; however, the risks posed by the launch phase of a new product or service are often acutely short term in nature—though potentially harboring long-term consequences. The most rational course is to view everything, short-term and long-term, through a single strategic lens so that both types of risk are considered. Indeed, an enterprise-wide view of risk tends to be highly inclusive. While it typically concentrates on risks that threaten the strategy, ERM also identifies, anticipates, and responds to operational, compliance, and reporting risks, all of which can impact the strategic success of the enterprise. This makes the holistic and proactive scope of ERM a valuable strategic tool.

Actually Managing Risk

While ERM takes a wide-angle view, it also identifies the top ten (give or take) risks to the organization and prioritizes mitigations. These highest-priority risks should figure most prominently in the strategy and business plan and should, therefore, be top of mind in the C-suite and boardroom. It is these risks that do most to determine the risk appetite of the enterprise. In this way, risk is truly managed—that is, weighed against and balanced against opportunity.

Central to managing risk is the so-called bowtie analysis. Each potential risk event (especially in the top ten category) should be analyzed regarding *causes* and *consequences*. Picture the risk itself as the knot of a bowtie. The wing to the left of the knot, labeled "causes," asks, "What would cause the risk event to happen?" and "What can we do to prevent the risk event from happening?" The wing to the right of the knot, labeled "consequences," asks, "What would be the consequences of its occurring?" and "What could we do to mitigate or minimize damage?"

Actually managing risk is, first and foremost, a top leadership responsibility, the buck stopping with the executive management and the board. These entities must understand and act upon the results of the ERM process, ensuring that the level of risk is within the boundaries of the enterprise's strategically determined risk appetite.

That company leadership takes proactive risk management has never been more important. The risk environment in most businesses is becoming increasingly complex even as the risks come at the enterprise in greater volume and with increasing velocity. Yet, simultaneously, the expectations of consumers, customers, regulators, investors, and employees for effective risk management continue to become increasingly demanding. For these reasons, the imperative to integrate risk management into strategy throughout the enterprise has never been clearer.

CHAPTER 17

KPIs

◈ ◈ ◈

"What gets measured gets done."

—PETER DRUCKER

THE FIRST PHILOSOPHER in the western tradition was a man named Thales of Miletus, who was born in what is today Turkey around 626 or 623 BC. He is often called the Father of Science because he took the bold step of abandoning mythology to explain the world and instead looked to nature to answer the most basic questions of existence. Mostly, he found the answers by measuring things, using geometry to calculate everything from the height of pyramids to the distance of ships from shore. In effect, he was looking for ways to establish objective fact— by which I mean truth existing apart from human perception, imagination, aspiration, or just plain wishful thinking. If you built a pyramid, you might declare it a thousand feet high, while your rival might deny it and claim it is only three hundred feet high. Find a method for creating a measurement independent of you, your rival, or anyone else, and you will arrive at fact. The Great Pyramid of Giza is (as it stands today) 454 feet high. Maybe your European friend insists it is just over 138 meters high, but that's fine since 454 feet is 138.379 meters. The units of measure are different, but each is standard and convertible to the other in a standard, objective way. More importantly, both the foot and the meter exist independently of human perception, aspiration, intention, motivation, imagination—whatever. They are lines and numbers on a yardstick or meter stick, standards on which there is general, nearly universal agreement.

Humans and the civilizations we build measure things and, more often than not, call those measurements reality, whereas everything else is a perception or an opinion.

Whether running a business, buying a business, or patronizing a business, you want to see the receipts. You want to see, evaluate, and compare key measurements. That is how you judge the realities of the business—its efficiency, value, success, and the deficiency or absence of these qualities.

"What gets measured gets done," Peter Drucker said. Sometimes, he is quoted as saying, "What gets measured gets improved." Based on my business experience, both these formulations are true, and I would suggest adding a third variation: *What gets measured is real. Everything else is subject to bias, private agenda, greed, hope, fear, and maybe a couple of thousand other conscious and unconscious motives.*

To provide reality-based leadership for any business, you must make frequent measurements. But what if you were walking down the street and saw a man in front of you carrying a yardstick and stopping to use it to measure one random object after another? I guess you would not go out of your way to ask him what he was doing or what he hoped to accomplish. I guess you'd give him a wide berth when you passed by, perhaps pausing only to check if the yardstick in his hand was complemented by a tinfoil hat upon his head.

Measure Strategically

Random measurement is, well, crazy, bonkers, unhinged, and, most of all, useless. Like everything else in a business that aims to conduct itself optimally, measurement must flow from strategy. It is important to measure, but it is even more important to measure the right things. The right things are those that have a strategic impact. Another way of putting this is to repeat one of the two variations on Drucker's formula: "What gets measured gets improved." Measure any strategic element that is capable of improvement. Remember Goldilocks, who was guilty of breaking into the home of a bear family of three? She found that one bowl of porridge was too cold, another too hot, but the third was *just right*. There are companies that do not make sufficient measurements. Some companies measure too much. Successful companies measure not for the sake of measurement but for the sake of creating improvement. This degree of measurement is *just right*.

Key Performance Indicators

KPIs are the critical quantifiable indicators of progress toward an intended—that is, strategic—result. KPIs bring into focus actions, processes, and assets capable of creating strategic and operational improvement. Muster the right KPIs and evaluate them, and you will have a sound analytical basis for making decisions about what matters most, namely the 20 percent of everything you do or make that drives 80 percent of your revenue. As a management tool, KPIs provide measurable desired levels of performance that serve as objective (because numerical) targets for a team, department, or company to hit by a set time—often a specified quarter. When a carmaker wants to persuade you that their vehicle outperforms the competition in acceleration, it does not take out an ad saying, "Our car is the fastest." Instead, the ad will quote a zero-to-sixty number and compare it to the zero-to-sixty numbers of its competitors. For car buyers with a need for speed, the zero-to-sixty figure is the KPI that determines whether they will purchase car X or its competitor, car Y.

Business managers often talk about "targets." This is useful—

up to a point. If your hobby is archery, you know it feels good to hit the bull's-eye in the middle of the target. If you are serious about your hobby, you practice and practice until you increase the rate at which you hit the bull's-eye. But no matter how committed you are to your hobby, once you release the bowstring and let fly the arrow, there is nothing on earth that you can do to improve that arrow's chances of hitting dead center on that particular flight. The trajectory is baked into your aim, the way you drew and released the bowstring, and, yes, wind conditions beyond your control. An arrow is not a smart weapon. It's a dumb weapon... aimed at a dumb target. In business, however, KPIs, taken together, constitute a smart target. By watching the KPIs, you can change the trajectory of your business. The reason is that individual KPIs or a sequence of KPIs can be used as key performance indicators and key leading indicators, which are predictors and even precursors of future success or the lack thereof. Recognize and measure the leading indicators, and you have a set of measurements that can drive desired impacts. You can change the trajectory of *this* arrow in mid-flight.

How do you validate the leading indicators you have identified? Easy. You look at the lagging indicators—the impact of any changes driven by the leading indicators. If the lagging indicators demonstrate measurable improvement, you have successfully read and acted upon the KPIs. This is not a gut feeling, the product of your Spidey sense, or an aching bunion. This is what the measured numbers tell you—and, incidentally, everyone else.

What Are Good KPIs?

Good KPIs have actionable meaning (the possibility of creating improvement) in the context of your goals and your business strategy. That said, there are some general common sense guidelines for identifying good KPIs. Good KPIs

- provide quantitative (and therefore objective) evidence of progress toward a desired result
- measure what you need to measure to better inform your decision-making
- offer a real comparison that allows you to gauge changes in performance over time
- track effectiveness, efficiency, quality, timeliness, compliance, governance, behavior, resource utilization, and economics
- track project performance as well as personnel performance
- are balanced between leading and lagging indicators

What Should You Measure?

Again, this varies with your business. If, say, you operate a specialty corner coffee shop, you will want to evaluate *inputs, outputs, process, outcomes,* and, perhaps, *project measures.*

Inputs: Coffee (including varieties, suppliers, quality, storage requirements, etc.), water, time (expressed either as hours or employee costs)

Outputs: The coffee you brew and serve (temperature, strength, style, taste, presentation, etc.)

Process: Procedures and equipment used

Outcomes: Sales and repeat sales (loyalty and customer satisfaction)

Project measures: Impact of any improvement projects, such as a special marketing campaign

Regardless of the size or nature of your business, each measure has its logic that contributes to creating an accurate movie of the progress of the business:

1. **Measuring inputs**—reveals the attributes (such as amount, type, and quality) of resources that are consumed in the production of *outputs*.

2. **Measuring processes**—reveals how the efficiency, quality, or consistency of the processes you use produce specific outputs. Evaluating a process may include evaluating controls on the process—for instance, tools or machines used, training required, etc.

3. **Measuring outputs**—tells you how much work is done and defines what that work produces.

4. **Measuring outcomes**—reveals the degree and effect of impacts. These may be divided into intermediate outcomes (for instance, customer brand awareness) and end outcomes (longer-term results, such as customer retention, sales trends, and so on).

5. **Measuring a project**—indicates the status of deliverables and milestone progress in major projects or initiatives.

Understand that inputs, processes, and outputs are operational measurements. Taken together, they have impacts on project scope. Outcomes, both intermediate outcomes and end outcomes, are measurements of strategic impact. It is, however, the combination of operational and strategic measurements that increases the strategic business intelligence of the enterprise.

Bear in mind that all businesses require strategic and operational KPIs. The strategic measures track progress toward strategic goals and thus focus on intermediate and end outcomes. Operational measures focus on operations and tactics to inform better decisions on a day-to-day basis. Improvements are incremental—but cumulative.

Add to these project measures, which focus on the effectiveness, impact, and overall progress of the project, risk measures, which are focused on risk factors that may pose threats to successful outcomes, and employee measures, which focus on the behaviors, skills, and performance needed to execute the strategy successfully.

Guiding Principles

KPIs are formulated within guiding principles prescribed by the company leadership. These are the strategic guardrails within which the company is to operate. The following is an example from a holding company (corporate level) and its operating companies:

Corporate Guiding Principles

1. Manage cash and control capital allocation
2. Oversee the implementation of the business strategy
3. Manage high-potential talent, especially in general management and finance

Operating Companies Guiding Principles

1. Do not go backward: maintain EBITDA and cash earnings returns
2. Lower break-even point
3. Generate higher EBITDA on incremental revenue (operating leverage)
4. Minimize capital expenditure
5. Minimize net working capital (payment terms are very important)
6. Retire unused, fixed assets aggressively
7. Grow from your business's strengths

What KPIs Look Like: Employees, Products, Customers

It can be helpful to think of KPIs as fitting into two broad categories. Some KPIs relate to employees, products, and customers, while others are strictly financial metrics. Within these two categories, you can formulate and use the KPIs that are most useful to your business. Consider employees, products, and customers as they relate to a manufacturing company. You will likely want to focus on at least four essential operational metrics: safety, quality, delivery, and productivity. Here is what KPIs for each of these metrics should tell you and how they should help you in a process of continual improvement:

Right to Grow Ratio: Diagnostic Indicator

What is It?
- Material Margin (MM) = Revenue − Purchases − Net Freight
- Total Employee Costs (TEC) include payroll, taxes, benefits, travel, commission, bonuses, insurance, etc.

What It Measures
- End-to-end efficiency of converting purchases to profits

How We Use It
- Point-in-Time & Trend
- Quantitative benchmark for "earning the right to grow"
- Informs Zero-Up objectives

Why It Matters
- Focuses attention on GM-controllable levers with near-term EBITDA impact

$$\text{Right to Grow Ratio} = \frac{\text{Material Margin}}{\text{Total Employee Cost}}$$

Fig. 17-01: Right to Grow Ratio: Diagnostic Indicator

Additional Employees, Products, and Customers KPIs

Depending on the needs and nature of your organization, you may want to create additional KPIs relating to employees, products, and customers in some or all of the following areas:

Talent Management

Look for KPIs that will enable you to assess the company's talent needs, especially by identifying gaps between your talent and the talent you need to achieve your goals. These metrics should guide a go-get plan to restructure a team or teams.

Product Line Simplification

Using 80/20, define KPIs that enable you to identify your most profitable stock-keeping units (SKUs) so that you can focus resources on these. Useful metrics in such 80/20 simplification would consider the life cycle of each product so that leadership can create a product portfolio that retains evergreens and cash cows while making room for rising stars among your SKUs. But endeavor to keep your simplification simple by ensuring that the KPIs you use identify, first and foremost, the products your customers are willing to pay for.

Innovation

KPIs are especially important for evaluating the impact of innovation. Innovation is not a value in itself. Rather, its value consists in the enhanced ability to offer better solutions to customers, to meet both their articulated and unarticulated needs, and to serve and even develop emerging markets with potential for rapid growth.

Some innovations are evolutionary, the result of incremental advances in technology or processes. Others (much rarer) are revolutionary. These are discontinuous—disruptive. In its day, the telephone was an evolutionary development from the telegraph. This device underwent a long evolutionary innovation process for many decades until it was suddenly disrupted by cellular technology, which created the revolutionary cell phone. The original bulky and costly cellular telephone handset improved through evolutionary innovation, which was itself disrupted by the emergence of the smartphone, initially in the form of the Apple iPhone.

What KPIs Look Like: Financial Metrics

All good KPIs are key. (Hey, "key" is right in their name.) But some key performance indicators are more key than others. All money is a number; therefore, money flow naturally makes for a set of key metrics. Here are financial metrics most industrial manufacturing organizations define as KPIs that provide targets to deliver or exceed:

Abbreviations used in Fig. 17-02a:

B/S: Balance sheet

CapEx: Capital expenditures

CRI: Cash return on investment

D&A: Depreciation
& amortization

DIOH: Days inventory on hand

DSO: Days sales outstanding

EBITDA: Earnings before
interest, taxes, depreciation,
and amortization

GM%: Gross margin percentage

M&A: Mergers and acquisitions

NPD: New product development

NWC: Net working capital

OpCo: Operating company

PD: Policy deployment

PP&E: Property, Plant,
and Equipment

PVM analysis: Price
volume mix analysis

SMP: Strategic
management process

WC: Working capital

	Metric	Description	Goal "What does good look like"	Rule of Thumb
Financial	**Revenue**	Sales	200 bps > market growth annually > 8 % annual organic target	Mid- to high- single- digits annual organic growth; exceed market growth
	EBITDA	Earnings before interest, taxes, depreciation and amortization	Improve EBITDA margin by > 100 bps annually	Low- to mid- double- digit annual growth Need a "path to 25%" and beyond
	Working Capital	Current assets – current liabilities	Mature < 20% of revenue Stable 20% - 25% New/expanding > 25%	Mature < 23% Stable 23% -27% New/expanding > 27%
	Capital Expenditure (CapEx)	Funds used to acquire or upgrade physical assets		
	Free Cash Flow	Net Income – (CapEx + ΔWC) + D&A	150% Net Income	Needs to be > NI 125% is okay
	Investment Leverage (IL)	EBITDA / Gross PP&E + WC		
	Cash Return on Investment (CRI)	Net Income + D&A – Maintenance CapEx / Gross PP&E + WC		

Fig. 17-02: What Financial KPIs look like: financial metrics

Operational Levers	Pay Attention To	Tools	Comments
Market & geography expansion, pricing, channel strategy / commissions, NPD, M&A	Order intake, backlog, deal pipeline, GM%, price/mix, % rev from target markets & geography; recurring revenue	Portfolio management, PVM analysis, M&A, NPD, SMP, PD	Needs to be higher than market. Shows we are taking share from competitors.
Growth, pricing, cost reductions, operating expenses	Margins, productivity, capacity utilization, quality, backlog, headcount	Lean, 80/20, talent, PD, operating budgets	Growth % needs to higher than revenue. Shows we are efficiently leveraging assets.
Payment terms and conditions, inventory levels	Primary working capital metrics: DSO, DPO, DIOH	80/20, lean, B/S ownership, daily meetings	Balance between providing good "service" and managing cash. Generally takes good process to fix
Growth: Sales Efficiency: Margins, NWC, Fixed Capital	Sales, SG&A, CapEx, Inventory, DSO	80/20, lean, PD & operating reviews, OpCo authority	It's the fuel that we use to grow the business; comprehensive assessment of performance. Cash is king!
			IL is used at the operating-company level.
			CRI is used at the enterprise level.

Gap Analysis

You can apply KPIs to a gap analysis, which compares actual performance with potential (usually desired) performance. When the KPIs indicate that the company is not using its resources, capital, or technology to achieve its full potential, you identify the gaps between actual performance and desired performance in six steps:

1. **Identify your current state**. At what level is the company currently operating? What products does it offer? What customers is it serving? What geographical locations does it penetrate? What benefits does it offer its employees? Quantitative information is important, of course, but qualitative input from all key stakeholders is also called for.

2. **Identify your future state**. What do you want to become? Compare this to where you are and then examine the resulting gaps. Set clear—typically quantified—goals accordingly.

3. **Identify the gaps**. Where are the shortfalls? What must you do to attain the goals representing your desired future state? By the way, you don't necessarily have to reinvent the wheel. Look at your competitors. What are they doing that you are not doing or that you could do better? What do you need in terms of product and service offerings, talent acquisition, growth, and M&A to reach the desired future state?

4. **Evaluate the proposed solutions**. This almost always means quantifying each so that the project change is measurable. Manufacturing costs are readily quantifiable, but so is customer satisfaction. What percentage of customers are satisfied? How much would improved customer service increase satisfaction? Gaps

in brand recognition (you want to increase recognition of your brand) often require more complex and creative solutions.

5. **Execute changes**. Decide on changes to make and implement them.

6. **Measure the impact of the changes**. Acting on the results of gap analysis is a feedback loop. Changes are made, their impact is measured, corrections are applied, and the direction may be pursued, altered, or altered radically.

Common Tools for Gap Analysis

SWOT is the most familiar gap analysis tool, but others are also commonly used.

SWOT analysis. "SWOT" is an acronym for *strengths*, *weaknesses*, *opportunities*, and *threats*, which pretty much covers the dimensions of any gap. The SWOT approach evaluates internal and external factors that require improvement or give the company an edge. SWOT analysis may guide a company to play to its strengths or may lead it to divert resources from those strengths to support the development of other capabilities. Profitable growth may require leaving your comfort zone, and if the company enjoys a wide market lead in a strong area, management may decide to redirect some resources to develop alternative opportunities. SWOT is also useful for probing an organization's weaknesses and gauging gaps with competitors. A careful analysis will help management decide if weaknesses can or should be overcome. Break-even analysis can be applied to determine whether the juice is worth the squeeze involved, for example, in making large capital investments.

SWOT analysis is not confined to identifying internal strengths and weaknesses. Some gaps result from external forces beyond the company's control. These include developments in technology, new government regulations, and other externals.

McKinsey 7s. In the 1970s, the McKinsey consulting firm proposed a gap analysis framework based on seven elements deemed essential to company performance. *Strategy, structure,* and *systems* are hard elements, while *shared values, skills, style,* and *staff* are the "soft elements." The 7s model assesses gaps in any of these areas, which management should address. The emphasis is on improving the coordination among the elements.

Fishbone Diagram. Also known as a cause-and-effect diagram or an Ishikawa diagram, fishbone diagrams are used to identify specific gaps and their impact. When a problem is identified, it is written down, and major categories are written on branches expanding away from the main problem. These break down the categories within the problem. Additional branches are added to these branches to identify why problems within each category exist. The result resembles a fishbone skeleton and can be surprisingly helpful in visually breaking down a complex problem into its constituent parts.

Nadler-Tushman Congruence Model. Developed in the 1980s to diagnose underperformance, the Nadler-Tushman model assesses the alignment and coordination of the chief components of an organization, such as culture, work, structure, and people. These four core principles receive data that is input (a company's strategy) as well as output (a company's performance). The end goal is to determine how each of the four components works together. Essentially, the model assumes that the input into an organization enters a matrix of culture, work, structure, and people. The output quality is a function of how the four components in the matrix interact. Using the model requires analyzing each component to identify misalignments among them. For instance, the company may have a brilliant staff but an organizational culture misaligned with them. It may have great technology in processes (work) but an outmoded bureaucratic culture that slows decision-making.

PEST Analysis. *PEST* stands for *political, economic, social,* and *technological* and identifies and assesses the external factors that create or exacerbate performance gaps. *PESTLE*, a variation on *PEST*, adds *legal* factors to the externals list. A common "external" that PEST analysis exposes is government regulation that adds expense to imports or exports.

Types of Gap Analysis

Gap analysis comes in various flavors because performance gaps occur in various areas and aspects of the business.

Market Gap Analysis. Also called product gap analysis, market gap analysis focuses on how customer needs may go unmet in a given market. The company that identifies markets and segments of markets in which product supply is insufficient to satisfy consumer demand has discovered a gap that is potentially worth filling. Tools to aid in market gap analysis include

- **Perceptual Mapping**, which diagrams the target-market consumer's perceptions of competing products in the marketplace
- **Product, Presence, Hit Rate Analysis (PPH)**. This analytical approach breaks down market share into quantifiable components of product (or service) coverage:
- P [product] x P [sales presence] x H [hit rate] = MS [market share]
- **Ansoff Matrix,** which is named after its originator, Igor Ansoff, who formulated it back in 1957. The matrix specifies present and potential products and markets (customers) for a business through four possible product-market combinations. This visual framework is intended to aid executives and marketers for future

business growth strategies based on levers and resources available to the company.

The Ansoff Matrix

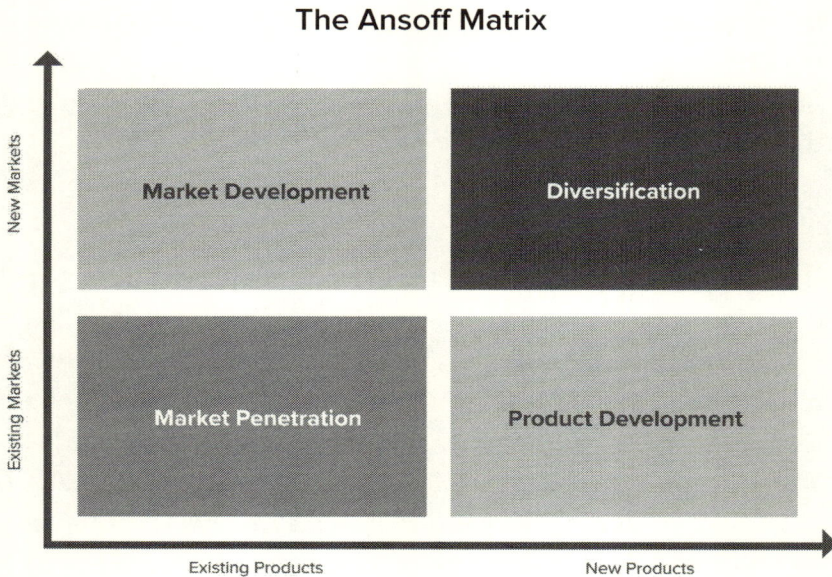

Fig. 17-03 The Ansoff Matrix. Credit: JaisonAbeySabu
CC By-SA 3.0

Strategic Gap Analysis, or performance gap analysis, is a formal performance review over a specified period during which the organization has followed a strategic plan. The analysis is an evaluation of the strategy. It is often used to assess the strategy by comparing the company's performance versus its competitors.

Financial/Profit Gap Analysis is a straightforward comparison with competitors regarding such financial metrics as pricing comparisons, margin percentages, overhead costs, revenue per labor, etc. The objective is to identify areas where a competitor is more financially efficient, determine why, and decide what features of the competitor's model may be worth emulating.

Skill Gap Analysis assesses any deficiency in knowledge and expertise among current personnel. Skill gaps may be addressed through training or new hires. It is also possible that the organization may decide not to compete in areas in which it is insufficiently staffed.

Compliance Gap Analysis assesses the degree to which the company efficiently operates within a set of external (government) regulations and how the cost of compliance can be reduced.

Product Development Gap Analysis is used to assess the fit of the company's new products with the marketplace, especially with respect to which features, benefits, and functions of proposed products will meet market demand and where they will fall short.

Break-Even Analysis should be part of formulating and implementing the results of any gap analysis. It calculates the amount that projected revenues resulting from closing a gap exceed the point at which expenses and revenue are equal.

Better Is Best

One of the lessons generations of elementary school teachers have drilled into generations of students is the grammatical concept of absolute, comparative, and superlative degrees. Teachers have often used this little jingle to get their point across:

> *Good, better, best—*
> *Never let it rest*
> *Until the good is better*
> *And the better best.*

This is a valid and useful lesson in grammar, but it is not a formula for doing business optimally. The "goal" of continuous improvement is to elevate *good* to *better* and *better* to even *better*. There is no *best* for the simple reason that the superlative degree spells the end of improvement. Set goals, achieve them, and then move them. Achieve more. *Best* is not a best practice because *better* is best.

Continuous improvement need not end.

Is this a frustrating and unfair case of moving the goalposts? No. Continuous improvement is absolute and objective, provided that it is measured by KPIs attained and not attained. The yardstick remains absolute, and the team is given credit for their improvement and held accountable for their lack of improvement. The last thing you want is to get too comfortable. Today's incumbent leader in any field is always painted with a target.

CHAPTER 18

PDCA: Feedback and Course Correction

"A stumble may prevent a fall."

—THOMAS FULLER, *Gnomologia*, 1732

HARRY S. TRUMAN was a member of one of the most exclusive clubs in American history. He became president not because he was elected to the office but because the man he served as vice president, Franklin Delano Roosevelt, died early in his unprecedented fourth term. FDR's sudden demise both grieved and terrified the American people. A senator from Missouri, Truman was widely mocked as "the senator from Pendergast" since he had been handpicked for the Senate by the notoriously corrupt Tom "Boss" Pendergast. Aside from that tarnished pedigree, Truman was not very well known nationally. Nor was he particularly charismatic. Terribly nearsighted, he wore wire-rim glasses and fussily tailored double-breasted suits (he had partnered in a haberdashery back home in Independence, Missouri), the combination of which somehow made him look short, even though he stood five foot ten. "I suppose I make a smaller appearance or something like that," he confessed. How could this small, nearsighted, Missouri political hack possibly take over for Roosevelt, who had brought the nation through and out of the Great Depression and led the United States as the linchpin of a great global military alliance in World War II?

If the American people were scared and dismayed, Truman did not sound all that confident himself. Immediately after being sworn in, he confessed to a gaggle of reporters: "When they told me yesterday what happened"—that President Roosevelt had succumbed to a cerebral hemorrhage—"I felt like the moon, the stars, and all the planets had fallen on me." Yet, famously, he immediately rose to the occasion in what proved to be a hard, lonely job.

He revealed the secret of his surprising success in "Making Up Your Mind," an essay in a collection of essays he asked his daughter, Margaret, to publish after he died. He explained in the essay that the presidency was nothing more or less than leadership, and leadership was nothing more or less than making up your mind, deciding what to do, and then doing it. He described the process straightforwardly:

First of all, the president has got to get all the information he can possibly get as to what's best for the most people in the country, and that takes both basic character and self-education. He's not only got to decide what's right according to the principles by which he's been raised and educated, but he also has to be willing to listen to a lot of people, all kinds of people, and find out what effect the decision he's about to make will have on the people. And when he makes up his mind that his decision is correct, he mustn't let himself be moved from that decision under any consideration. He must go through with that program and not be swayed by the pressures that are put on him by people who tell him that his decision is wrong. If the decision is wrong, all he has to do is get some more information and make another decision, because he's got to have the ability to change his mind and start over. That's the only way in the world a man can carry on as chief executive.

A Leader Leads Through Decision

President Truman made some of the most consequential decisions in history, starting with the decision to use atomic weapons to end World War II and continuing through the momentous decisions to order the racial integration of the US Armed Forces (an act that inaugurated the great postwar Civil Rights Movement) and to implement the Marshall Plan to rescue a devasted Europe from the threats of starvation, famine, and Soviet conquest. This, in turn, determined a victorious Cold War strategy of "containing" the spread of totalitarian communism without provoking a third world war. Decisions such as these would overwhelm anyone. Truman approached them straightforwardly and rationally:

1. Get all the information you can get.
2. Use your background, consult your moral compass, solicit opinions from a diverse range of people, and listen to those most affected by your decision.
3. Make your decision.
4. Follow through, and don't be swayed.
5. If the decision is wrong, get more information and make another decision.
6. Be prepared and willing to change your mind based on results.
7. Start over with a new decision.
8. This process is the "only way" a leader can make effective decisions.

Get data, analyze the data, seek input from an array of people (especially those who will be most affected by the decision at hand), act, don't heed the nay-sayers but monitor results, and be open to changing your mind if necessary. We can simplify the description this way: *Make the best decision you can make. Act on it. If it doesn't work, get more information and make a new decision. Act on it. Keep monitoring. Rinse and repeat.*

Business advances only through decision-making. A business *may* fail if the decisions are bad, but it is certain to fail if no decisions are made or if they are acted upon indecisively. Bad decisions can be corrected with good or at least better decisions, provided that the leaders of the enterprise are willing to change their minds. The courage, will, and energy to change your mind is essential to evaluating decisions and deciding whether (and how) to make new decisions. The best way to evaluate the effect of your decisions is to create a periodic feedback loop that runs backward from the business plan to the situation assessment. With a situation assessment freshly informed by new information, the leader guides the enterprise through constructing a modified or, sometimes, entirely new strategic framework and, using this, creates a new or modified business plan.

PDCA

I doubt President Truman ever heard of PDCA—*plan, do, check, act*—but had someone shown it to him, he would have recognized it as his theory and practice of leadership. The same holds true for any effective business leader or manager. You might look at your KPIs and not much like what you see. Sometimes, the path to improvement is obvious, with the answers in the numbers. But what do you do if you just don't know what to do?

You *plan, do, check, and act*—PDCA.

PDCA is also known as the Shewhart cycle or Deming wheel—for a good reason. Walter Shewhart was a statistician who originally developed the PDCA concept during the 1930s. Two decades later, the great American engineer, statistician, and all-around management consultant W. Edwards Deming popularized PDCA in his pioneering work on quality control during the 1950s. This simple sequence has been widely and effectively used to implement the revelations of KPI and can affect major performance breakthroughs and incremental improvements in projects and processes. The PDCA steps are disclosed in the very name of the practice.

Plan. Begin by understanding the problem requiring remedy or the opportunity promising improvement. Gaining this understanding begins with five steps.

1. **Strategic link**: first, determine how improving the issue in question contributes to achieving the business strategy.
2. **Current State**: next, dive deeply into the issue until you see all the problems and opportunities.
3. **Future State**: having inventoried the current state, envision your desired future state. That is, clearly define change by setting goals or targets that must be achieved to realize the business value you need to gain.
4. **Identify the Team**: assemble a team that will provide multiple perspectives on the issue.
5. **Leadership Support**: secure agreement among leadership to invest the needed personnel, time, and other resources to resolve the issue, solve the problems, and realize the opportunities.

After completing the five steps above, you are prepared to identify potential causes of the issue. Begin with divergent thinking to establish as many potential causes as possible. Don't inventory symptoms. List possible causes. Seek feedback and multiple viewpoints from people outside of the team. Next, set about collecting and analyzing data to determine which of the potential causes of the issue are worth pursuing. Use convergent thinking to reach this short list.

Next, focus on your short list of causes to identify

countermeasures. This requires shifting back to divergent thinking to develop an expansive list of possible actions to address root causes. Switch to convergent thinking to prioritize the items on your list by criteria important to achieving the future state you have defined. Filter these items by recognizing resource limitations.

Now you are ready to prepare an action plan. Begin by blocking out a high-level plan, which should give you an understanding of actions to advance you toward your target. Flesh out the high-level plan to create a detailed plan. Essentially, break down the high-level elements into multiple tasks or steps.

Once you have an actionable plan, seek leadership support and agreement to invest time, money, and other resources needed to implement the plan.

Do: Execute the plan—implement the countermeasures—and collect data on results. Use the visual management techniques discussed earlier to track and measure progress and impact.

Check: Evaluate the results produced by implementing the countermeasures. Assess the execution of the plan. Your objective is to verify your hypothesis for the countermeasure and to evaluate the timeliness of realizing the benefit. Above all, learn from the result to improve the team's problem-solving capabilities. What worked? What did not work? And why?

Act: Determine the next steps in executing the business strategy or plan through continuous improvement. Based on the results—degree of improvement or degree of lack of improvement—decide what to do next. For successful countermeasures, disseminate them to other processes or areas. For countermeasures that fail to produce change, continue collecting results and reevaluate the nature and status of the problem or issue.

An Enduring Lesson from Toyota

Ultimately, the feedback loop is driven by one obvious, abundantly straightforward question: "Are we achieving our plan?" The answer to this question is expressed in performance metrics, results, and whether prioritized actions are occurring as planned. Determining to what degree the company is successfully executing its strategy requires analysis.

In the late 1960s and into the 1970s, Sakichi Toyoda, founder of Toyota Industries, created the so-called Five Whys. This is an elegantly simple method of getting to the root cause of problems and issues that interfere with the successful implementation of a business plan. The idea is that most problems can be solved by asking why five times.

Say, for example, there is a water puddle on the floor.

The question *Why?* prompts an obvious answer: *the overhead pipe is leaking*.

Asked a second time, *Why?* goes deeper toward a root cause: *the water pressure in the pipe is too high*.

The third asking of *Why?* prompts the conclusion *the control valve is faulty*.

Asked a fourth time, *Why?* yields *our control valves have not been tested*.

In the fifth repetition, *Why?* elicits *the control valves have not been listed on the maintenance schedule*. With this, the root cause has been discovered, and the discovery implies the appropriate action: *Put a control valve inspection on the maintenance schedule. Do it now.*

Toyota also created another useful problem-solving tool called the A3 process. (Why A3? Because 11-by-17-inch paper, known as A3 paper, was traditionally used at Toyota to jot down ideas, plans, and goals during an "A3 process.")

1. **Begin by identifying the problem or need.**
2. **Once the problem/need is identified,** determine the current state of the situation by observing and documenting the work processes involved. Next, gather the team around

a whiteboard and chart each production process step.

3. Quantify the size of the problem.

For example, "X number of customer deliveries that are late." Or "X number of manufacturing errors that occurred last quarter." Present the data graphically.

With the current state of the situation quantified, begin a root-cause analysis. Again, the analysis is generated through questions such as

- What information do we need to work more effectively?
- Where are the delays in the process? Where are they the longest?
- Where are we failing to communicate adequately?

Identify the pain points in the operation and apply the Five Whys to dig down to the root causes. With root causes identified, take these next steps:

1. **Formulate countermeasures—changes in your processes—to address root causes.** These include changing your processes to move the organization closer to ideal by addressing root causes. These changes should begin by specifying the intended outcome and then laying out a plan for achieving it. Review the connections and coordination between people responsible for steps in the process and clarify or change these as needed. Ferret out loops and delays in the process.

2. **Define your target state.** Having formulated the necessary changes in the process, define your target state with a process map, which notes where the changes in the process are occurring so they can be observed and evaluated.

3. **Develop a revised implementation plan**. This should include a task list to get the process changes in place, a roster of who is responsible for what, and due dates for task completion.

4. **Develop a follow-up plan, including predicted outcomes.** This important step allows the teams to verify improvement. If improvement is absent, the teams must review whether the implementation plan was executed, the target condition was realized, and the expected results were achieved.

5. **Once the A3 process is satisfactorily completed, the results should be reported so that they can be used by all teams involved in executing the improvement plan.** Everyone needs to buy into the new or modified processes. Consensus must be built and verified.

When buy-in is obtained, it is time to implement the new process. However, remember that implementation is not the final step in the improvement process. The results must be evaluated. If they vary substantially from expectations, research the matter to find out why. Use this feedback to make further changes in your processes until they attain all the strategic goals that have been set.

Profitable growth is strategic growth, growth that grows profitability. As strategic growth, profitable growth requires continuous improvement, and continuous improvement requires a strategic focus on profitable growth. It turns out that what may look like an upward-inflecting line on the chart of a successful business is actually the result of a feedback loop driven by the rhythmic process of *plan, do, check, act.*

CHAPTER 19

A Final Word on Leadership: The Rule of Three

● ● ●

"Omne trium perfectum is a trio of Latin words that convey a simple overarching philosophy: 'everything that comes in threes is perfect.'"

—LESLIE CRANFORD, "Three Nontraditional Students and Sisters Complete Journey to Graduation," *Texas Tech Today*, April 10, 2023

EVERY BUSINESS NEEDS a leader. But when your mother told you that two heads are better than one, she was only two-thirds right. If you are going to run your business with PGOS, you must have three key leaders.

I'd like to tell you that nothing is magical about the number three, but it materializes—as if by magic—in so many human practices and endeavors that you often hear about a *rule of three*. Don't take my word for it. Look it up. Call me lazy, but Wikipedia has compiled a convenient list. There is a rule of three in the fields of

- aviation and aeronautics, governing descent in terms of altitude vs. travel distance
- C++ programming, a rule of thumb concerning class method definitions

- computer programming, a rule of thumb about code defactoring
- hematology, a rule of thumb for checking the accuracy of blood counts
- mathematics, a method of arithmetic
- medicinal chemistry, a rule of thumb for lead-like compounds
- statistics, a rule for calculating a confidence limit in the absence of observable events
- survival, prioritizing survival steps
- the Trinity (Father, Son, and Holy Ghost), central to most Christian denominations
- Wicca, a rule stating that whatever energy a person puts into the world comes back to him or her times three

There is even a rule of three for writers, holding that three entities or events in a piece of writing are more effective than any other quantity. Think *Three Little Pigs*, *Goldilocks and the Three Bears*, and *Three Musketeers*. Many, probably most, modern plays have three acts, and the most memorable slogans tend to consist of three words or phrases, no more, no fewer: *Life, Liberty, and the pursuit of Happiness*; *stop, look, and listen*; *stop, drop, and roll*; *turn on, tune in, drop out*; *Snap, Crackle, and Pop*; *government of the people, by the people, for the people*.

Julius Caesar also describes his generalship in the Gallic Wars (58-50 BC) with just three words: *Veni, Vidi, Vici*—"I came, I saw, I conquered." Speaking of Caesar, he was a founding member of the First Triumvirate, which, along with the Second Triumvirate, was the most famous three-person leadership group in history. The First Triumvirate was formed in 60 BC by Caesar, Pompey, and Crassus to share absolute power over the Roman Republic.

Memo to future triumvirates: the thing about absolute power is that it really cannot be shared.

By 55 BC, the First Triumvirate was starting to crumble. Two years later, Crassus was killed when he invaded Parthia, which responded with extreme prejudice. This briefly made Caesar and Pompey more cooperative with one another, but then Caesar started a civil war in 49 BC, defeated Pompey the next year, and Pompey fled to Egypt, where a Roman officer serving in the Egyptian army lopped off his head. Caesar? He enjoyed sole absolute rule of Rome for just under four years before he was stabbed to death on the Ides of March, 44 BC.

As for the Second Triumvirate (Mark Antony, Lepidus, and Octavian), it dissolved in a new civil war after three years, leaving Octavian as the sole ruler of Rome. He soon ditched the Roman Republic and founded the Roman Empire, which he ruled as Caesar Augustus from January 16, 27 BC to August 19, AD 14.

So, the rule of three kind of broke down in ancient Rome. Why?

Both triumvirates had the right number of players, three each, but the mojo of three, it turns out, is not exclusively in the quantity. It's also in the things and the people involved. If your grocery list has three items—an onion, an apple, and a can of kitchen cleanser—you don't come home with three onions and call the shopping spree a success. Each of the triumvirs in the two Roman triumvirates wanted to be *the* supreme leader, the top banana, the big tuna. They wanted the same exclusive job. This proved to be a formula for failure and fatal conflict. Far from discrediting the idea of a leadership triumvirate, it simply demonstrates how not to put a three-person team together. The United States government, which has endured for nearly 250 years, is a triumvirate, with power distributed among the Executive, Legislative, and Judicial branches, each of which has its own critical leadership domain and commands powers that complement, check, and balance the powers of the other branches.

In this book, we've talked about processes and tools. Before we say goodbye, we'd better talk about people. All you have to know about *people* is that there is no business without them. About one category of people—leaders—you need to know a bit more. I *believe* that every great business *benefits* not from a single great leader but three. I *know* that any business that chooses to apply PGOS to their organization *needs* three great leaders. They are a visionary, a prophet, and an operator.

The Visionary

The visionary is the final decision-maker within the organization, which almost always means the CEO. Within the triumvirate and the entire organization, the visionary has absolute authority. She or he makes decisions and issues directives to other executives and managers, who are held accountable for acting on those directives. While the decisions of the visionary should be firm and unambiguous, they are, like everything else in any company, dedicated to continuous improvement and subject to further decisions that may modify some or all of the CEO's preceding decisions. Recall what President Truman wrote about presidential decisions. When the president "makes up his mind that his decision is correct, he mustn't let himself be moved from that decision under any consideration. He must go through with that program and not be swayed by the pressures that are put on him by people who tell him that his decision is wrong." Of course, Truman knew that any of his decisions could prove wrong, but he had an answer for that: "If the decision is wrong, all [the president] has to do is get some more information and make another decision, because he's got to have the ability to change his mind and start over."

"Visionary" has certain connotations. Some people hear the word and think of a soothsayer, a person who has visions and sees the future, often while in a kind of dream or trance state. This is not the vision *you* need. *Your* visionary understands the present state and, with imagination and wisdom, leads the planning for a future state. In this respect, people as different as

Steve Jobs and Jack Welch come to mind.

But we need to get more specific.

Air traffic controllers carry out an incredibly demanding job of safely and efficiently coordinating takeoffs, approaches, and landings at busy airports. They continuously monitor highly dynamic situations with many moving parts, calmly and concisely communicating with pilots, telling them what actions to take and when to take them. How do the controllers do it? How do they keep all those moving parts moving safely and efficiently? How do they hold up under such pressure? To put it more bluntly, how do they keep the planes from crashing into each other?

Any air traffic controller will tell you that the secret to avoiding midair catastrophe is to start out by doing something called "getting the picture." The most successful chess players and military commanders possess a knack for rapidly understanding the situation on the board or battlefield before them. The French call this coup *d'oeil*, which may be translated as a "glance that takes in a comprehensive view." Napoleon had it, General Ulysses S. Grant had it, General George S. Patton had it—and every successful air traffic controller has it. It is the *picture*—a real-time vision of each aircraft in relation to every other aircraft within a certain space. Every decision the air traffic controller makes and every instruction given to each pilot is made or given within the frame of this "picture."

The visionary the PGOS-driven business needs must possess the core competence of an air traffic controller and the ability to assess the business at any point in time but always within the frame of the "picture," the dynamic context and environment in which the profitable growth strategy is deployed. Because all the parts of this picture are always in motion, the visionary must be agile and focused. Time creates pressure on decision-makers, to be sure, but it also provides the possibility and the space for maneuver. Deploying a strategic business plan within the guardrails of the 80/20 principle transforms static strategy into dynamic deployment. The clock is running. This applies pressure, but it also means that your goal is not some abstract static *state* of *perfection* but a real-life *process* of *progress*.

The Prophet

The first company I was hired to run (by the private equity firm that had purchased it) consisted of a conglomerate of decentralized businesses specializing in various medical, technical, and industrial niche components and applications. In principle, 80/20 thinking guided this decentralized company. In practice, however, many unit presidents tended to go their own way. We brought in outside consultant trainers to inculcate and disseminate 80/20 more uniformly across all the subsidiary companies, but, competent though these hired hands were, the results they produced were wildly uneven. I realized that we needed to fully internalize our 80/20 processes, and the only way to do this was to bring it totally in-house.

What we needed, I said, was a prophet.

The prophet is a leader—often, but not necessarily, the COO—who has the knowledge and know-how to interpret the Rosetta Stone and thereby implement the vision of the visionary. By "implement," I mean training, coaching, and mentoring others throughout the organization to execute the company strategy. Unless you have a prophet who is integral with and organic to the organization, you will find that your executives, managers, and other key personnel will regress from alignment on the strategy and instead begin to practice what they individually believe is right. The result is suboptimization, the effects of which are analogous to trying to run a car without oil.

Many businesses these days have a position or set of positions called "evangelist" or "chief evangelist." These individuals lead in promoting a product, service, or range of products and services to grow the company's customer base. While this is not the job of the individual I call the prophet, I am inclined to use the word in its nonbusiness, general sense. The first evangelist was St. John, known as St. John the Evangelist, who was one of the four writers of the Gospels. Ever since him, a person who seeks to convert others to Christianity, mainly by preaching, has been called an "evangelist." What I mean by prophet is an evangelist in this sense: a propagator of the faith.

The unifying structuring principle of a PGOS-driven company does resemble the idea of a religion, namely the Gospel according to Pareto. Religions are based on the notion that there is only *one right way*. PGOS also holds that there is only *one right way*: to embrace a strategy that focuses on, allocates resources to, and ultimately executes the roughly 20 percent of actions that create roughly 80 percent of the company's revenue. A great example of a company that has mastered the use of 80/20 thinking is Illinois Tool Works (NYSE: ITW). In the early 1980s, ITW faced rising costs and decreasing profitability. Company leadership decided to use the 80/20 principles to drive a complete overhaul of its policies, techniques, and rules of operation. Over twenty-five years, ITW not only perfected its application of the 80/20 rule, but the company enjoyed annual shareholder returns of 19 percent without fail—many times by acquiring companies and applying the principles of 80/20 to them. That's one profitable Gospel.

Unlike virtually all religions, however, PGOS preaches a *one right way* subject to continuous revision with the goal of incremental improvement. As Gospels go, it is supremely agile. As a religion, it is a resilient process rather than a rock of ages. The prophet in a PGOS-driven enterprise evangelizes for total understanding of the core strategy, total commitment, and complete coordinated engagement with the other true believers in the company. But the prophet also honors and enables change and adaptation within the core strategy.

The prophet is not the author of the Holy Writ—that is the role of the visionary—but is its keeper, interpreter, and evangelist. Like any other evangelist, our prophet is also charged with transforming others within the company into evangelists. The prophet, who possesses the PGOS knowledge, understanding, insight, and tools, shares these throughout the organization.

The Operators

The operators are the leaders who actually run the business on a day-to-day level. Typically, "operator" corresponds to the corporate title of president, though this is not always the case. In the kind of conglomerated businesses I have run during my career, the operators have been the presidents of segments or operating companies. In contrast to the visionary, they don't set the strategy, but they are charged with implementing and executing it within their companies or segments.

The operators know their companies, but they are not the source of the overall strategy (that is the job of the visionary) and they are neither the keepers nor masters of the tools by which that strategy is implemented (that is the domain of the prophet). They know and run their companies, and they must be thoroughly evangelized on the strategic vision and on the means and tools to employ to ensure that their business is aligned with the strategy and meets or exceeds all its strategic goals.

The Point Is, It Works

Having a prophet among you creates profit. (Yes, it's a pun. And yes, it's intentional.) How important is a prophet? At Phoenix, we were able to take sales from $700 million to over $1 billion and profit from $70 million to $175 million in 863 days! That's 150 percent growth in EBITDA, and anybody with eyes to see and ears to hear would call that a real impact.

But recall the proverb, "Where there is no vision, the people perish." PGOS will deliver extraordinary results only if the complete triumvirate—visionary, prophet, and operator—is present and active in the organization. The prophet guides the execution of the vision throughout the organization, aligning the company on the strategy and applying 80/20. Without a visionary, however, there is no vision. Without a vision, there can be no prophet. The operators take their direction from the visionary and apply it with the prophet's instruction, guidance, and mentoring. Without the operators, the work of the visionary and the prophet comes to nothing.

I do not ask that you take on faith the efficacy of the rule of three in running the profitable growth operating system. I have personally seen it turn companies around time and again. Just remember that, as with a joint stool, it takes all three legs to stand.

Without the visionary (CEO), the team would not have a clear goal. Everyone would be firing unaimed arrows, which never miss yet hit who knows what. The operators would do things the way they have always been done and focus on whatever interested them, not on what was important to the company. Without the prophet, the team would lack a clear roadmap to achieve the visionary's goal. Without the operators, neither the visionary nor the prophet would have anything to do. The magic of three here is that the sum of the parts is greater than the whole. I think the 150 percent growth in EBITDA in 863 days speaks for itself.

PGOS is a time-tested set of simple tools and processes that foster a common culture, creating value for all stakeholders: customers, employees, suppliers, and shareholders. Under the leadership of visionary, prophet, and operator, PGOS enables business owners and management teams to identify challenges to their business operations and create clear, simple, actionable plans to increase the productivity of assets, increase profits, and make better decisions at every level of an organization. It works.

INDEX

f7207406-e1ea-439e-b3df-89a0f6479f15R01